D0097427

"A compelling and accomplished memoir recounting the dissolution of the sixties and the beginning of the modern, more cynical era that followed, *The Fine Wisdom and Perfect Teachings of the Kings of Rock and Roll* candidly describes Mark Edmundson's journey as a lost twenty-something seeking meaning through sex, drugs, Marxism, rock and roll, and ultimately, teaching."

—Philipp Meyer, author of *American Rust*

"Mark Edmundson doesn't just chronicle, he channels, the epoch of rock. With sentences that sometimes astonish, he makes us feel its hopes, its confusions, its genuine revelations. Edmundson frames the glories of the 1970s and their latter-day reckonings in a working life: concert security dude, cabbie, bouncer. These jobs provide him critical lenses on a succession of cultural moments, and on the never-ending task of becoming an adult."

—Matthew Crawford, author of *Shop Class as Soulcraft*

"*The Fine Wisdom and Perfect Teachings of the Kings of Rock and Roll* has alert, rueful-earnest prose . . . a nice retrospective feel for youthful appetites (more metaphysical than sensual). . . . Edmundson may lean more toward Woody Allen than Warren Zevon, but in his wide-eyed receptivity to whatever fortune comes his way, his youthful self might have stepped out of a dozen early Jackson Browne tunes. . . . Through his droll quest-romance peregrinations, set on his eager way by the Stones and *The Faerie Queene*, Edmundson has the alacrity and dumb pluck of a tenderfoot prospecting for gold. . . . [It's] a young man's version of *An Education*."

—Howard Hampton, *New York Times Book Review*

about the author

MARK EDMUNDSON teaches at the University of Virginia, where he is University Professor. A prizewinning scholar, he has published a number of works of literary and cultural criticism, including *Why Read?*; *Literature Against Philosophy, Plato to Derrida*; and *Teacher: The One Who Made the Difference*. He has also written for such publications as the *New Republic*, the *New York Times Magazine*, *The Nation*, and *Harper's*.

ALSO BY MARK EDMUNDSON

The Death of Sigmund Freud:
   The Legacy of His Last Days

Why Read?

Teacher: The One Who Made the Difference

Nightmare on Main Street:
   Angels, Sadomasochism, and the Culture of Gothic

Literature Against Philosophy, Plato to Derrida:
   A Defence of Poetry

Wild Orchids and Trotsky:
   Messages from American Universities

Towards Reading Freud: Self-Creation in Milton, Wordsworth,
   Emerson, and Sigmund Freud

THE FINE WISDOM
AND PERFECT TEACHINGS
OF THE KINGS OF
ROCK AND ROLL

(a memoir)

Mark Edmundson

HARPER ⬤ PERENNIAL

NEW YORK • LONDON • TORONTO • SYDNEY • NEW DELHI • AUCKLAND

HARPER ● PERENNIAL

A hardcover edition of this book was published in 2010 by HarperCollins Publishers.

HarperCollins books may be purchased for educational, business, or sales promotional use. For information please write: Special Markets Department, HarperCollins Publishers, 10 East 53rd Street, New York, NY 10022.

Epigraph on page ix reprinted with the permission of Scribner, a Division of Simon & Schuster, Inc., from THE COLLECTED WORKS OF W. B. YEATS, VOLUME I THE POEMS, REVISED edited by Richard J. Finneran. Copyright © 1933 by The Macmillan Company; copyright renewed © 1961 by Bertha Georgie Yeats. All rights reserved.

FIRST HARPER PERENNIAL EDITION PUBLISHED 2011.

Designed by Eric Butler

The Library of Congress has catalogued the hardcover edition of this book as follows:

Edmundson, Mark, 1952 –
    The fine wisdom and perfect teachings of the kings of rock and roll : a memoir / by Mark Edmundson. – 1st ed.
        p.   cm.
    Summary: "A coming-of-age memoir about one man's miscues and false starts as he enters the world after college and attempts to answer the timeless question of who he is, while contemplating what role music, love, work, drugs, money, and books will play in his life"—Provided by publisher.
    ISBN 978-0-06-171347-7 (hardback)
    1. Edmundson, Mark, 1952—Knowledge and learning. 2. Edmundson, Mark, 1952—Books and reading. 3. Edmundson, Mark, 1952—Drug use. 4. College graduates—New York (State)—New York—Biography. 5. College teachers—United States—Biography. 6. Rock music—1961–1970. 7. New York (N.Y.)—Biography. I. Title.
    CT275.E337A3   2010
    378.1'2092—dc22
    [B]   2009049488

ISBN 978-0-06-171349-1 (pbk.)

11   12   13   14   15   ID/RRD   10   9   8   7   6   5   4   3   2   1

To Liz & Matthew & Willie
Still Rolling

A living man is blind and drinks his drop.
What matter if the ditches are impure?
What matter if I live it all once more?
Endure that toil of growing up;
The ignominy of boyhood; the distress
Of boyhood changing into man;
The unfinished man with his pain
Brought face to face with his own clumsiness.

—Yeats, "A Dialogue of Self and Soul"

Might as well jump. Jump!

—Van Halen, "Jump"

CONTENTS

The Fine Wisdom and Perfect Teachings
of the Kings of Rock and Roll

BEGINNINGS

(hot shits)

Beauty brought the Beast of Rock and Roll to my door, and he was something to see. He was six feet three inches tall at least, and he had a pudding of a belly, but his shoulders and back looked to be rammed with rhino strength. His beard, an Amish-style affair, wispy and auburn-colored, wound around the edge of his face. He had a turned-up nose—when he stared at me, I could see the nostrils, broad and cavernous— and small eyes that were laser lights of intelligence behind his thick glasses. He was looking a little abashed. It was as though Beauty had clapped an invisible chain on him and pulled him down the corridor, largely against his will. It was nearly three o'clock in the morning. Beauty, whose name was Deidre Brown and who was lovely and softly dignified, looking as she did like one of the ancient Muses, had clearly had enough. She couldn't handle him anymore. Her eyes were bloodshot. His eyes were bloodshot, too, and despite looking abashed, he was obviously still amok with energy. Rays of rogue light came at me from the tiny hyperintelligent peepers.

"Mark," said Deidre, "this is my friend Pelops Kazanjian. He's brilliant. You'll interest each other. I have to go to bed." She dropped Pelops's invisible chain and walked away. "Pelops," I thought, trying to commit his name to memory, "sounds like 'Never Stops.'"

This was in the spring of 1974 at Bennington College, from which I was about to graduate. (A mistake, I was told time after time. You're in heaven. Why leave?) I was pounding away on my senior thesis the midmorning that Pelops arrived; I was writing about Thomas Pynchon, or trying to. *V.* and *The Crying of Lot 49* had mesmerized me, and I had to figure them out. In only a couple of weeks, the thesis was due. Then I was going to graduate, and what I'd do with all my hard-won literary knowledge I had no idea.

Pelops strode into my room. He stared at my bookcase with the laser eyes. He saw novels, poems, plays, some lit crit. He did not approve. "Bourgeois piffle," he announced. "I mean no offense. But this is last-gasp stuff. The age of the oppressors is almost over. These books are their death rattle." As he spoke he became agitated. He strode up and down my small room like a Visigoth in a sacristy.

"Come," he said. "Confined spaces are not what I need. Come, we must walk! Come, we must march!"

March we did. For the next three hours and more, we conducted a forced maneuver through the Bennington College campus. We went at a furious pace. Pelops orated. I listened and tried to keep up.

Pelops had, he informed me, come from New York City to visit with Deidre. The city was oppressing him, but what he had forgotten was that in general the country oppressed him more. He referred to the country as latifundia, as I knew Karl Marx did (I'd had a course on his writings); Pelops spoke, also in Marx's mode, about "the idiocy of rural life." "It dulls one's sense of alienation," he proclaimed. "And in the beginning this is an acceptable thing. Everyone needs a rest. But this dulling eventually turns into a torpor that is not productive. I prefer an urban setting; it sharpens the sense of injustice. But here I must walk. I must walk and I must talk. It can't be otherwise." And then his voice turned plaintive. "Please come with me," he said. "I love Deidre, but I think I have completely worn her out."

I had never heard anyone talk this way before. It was not quite like he was addressing a rally. It was more as if he thought he was in the presence of a future biographer who was primed to hear memorable sentences and who also needed some political education.

During our forced march, which did not end until after sunrise, I learned many things. I learned that Pelops lived uptown in New York City (way uptown, in a place white people rarely dared to go) and was a student at NYU, where his father was an esteemed professor of art history. But Pelops had no time for art. Pelops loaded his curricular plate with more substantial stuff. He was enrolled to the tune of about twenty credits in courses that would enhance his powers as a radical-left intellectual. He was taking Russian, and next term he would be beginning Chinese. He took courses with the left-wing seers on the faculty, Marxist interpreters of the historical tea leaves. But he also signed up for classes with the reactionaries in order to tussle with them and sharpen his dialectical powers. "They're actually more useful," he told me.

3 •

"They illustrate all the forms of political error and teach one the tactics of mental combat." Then he told me, in a whisper, as though here in the Vermont countryside someone, from the left or the right, might be tracking his utterances, "Also, they're sometimes smarter than the true leftists. A good heart and a good head do not always go together."

While Pelops discoursed, we covered the campus, as though we were inspecting its terrain for a future guerrilla strike. We trudged past apple orchards, where the trees were not quite in bloom; they looked like scraggly souls in torment, Dante-esque sufferers raising their pained limbs in agony against the slowly brightening sky; we hopped stone walls, laid in place many decades past and pondered, probably, by Robert Frost, who'd been a poet in residence; we considered the tiny circle of cottages by the bridge, some of which had lights still burning. Bennington teachers were avant-garde creators, and there in the houses were being concocted long unrhymed and perhaps unreasoned poems, postsymphonic symphonies, and sculptures designed to evoke no object in existence now or ever. Pelops looked the place over. He made pronouncements. He said that the college, with its fixation on art and the new (always the new), was reactionary and pointless. He asked me what someone with my high intelligence—which I'd proved exclusively by being able to listen to him in almost complete silence for the past couple of hours—was doing in this bin of aesthetic poseurs and intellectual acrobats.

He understood from Deidre that I had working-class origins. This was more or less true, I admitted. While I was young, my father had been a short-order cook, though he'd risen a little in the world since. So, Pelops wanted to know, what was I doing betraying my class?

This got my back up. "What the hell should I do? Got any bright ideas?" I was going to graduate in a month, and I had made no plans for the future. My classmates all said that they had made no plans either. But this, I would come to see, was not quite true.

"We could go to Cuba," Pelops said. "We could labor in the fields. We could sing the songs of Fidel." What Pelops meant, I learned, was that we could head to the island with the Venceremos Brigade, foreigners who showed up in Cuba at harvest time and helped to cut the cane.

It was my turn to orate. I pointed out to Pelops that my family, perhaps unlike his, had been involved with cane cutting and its equivalents for many generations. In Ireland and Canada and then in America, we'd been peat slicers and plowmen and factory hands and dockworkers. My brother Phil and I had tacitly agreed between us that we were taking a generation off. No more forced labor for the Edmundsons.

Pelops took this in. He was not unimpressed. "Then what do you intend to do when they present you with your diploma?"

I told him that I had absolutely no idea. I thought that I might go back to Boston, where I was from, and see what might turn up.

"I suspect, Edmundson," he said, "that you will have to wait for a long time."

I admitted that this might be so. I asked him what he did for a living. How did he put food (and then, by the looks of things, more food) on the table?

"I work," Pelops said proudly, "in the music business. I work in rock and roll."

Rock and roll: the words glowed for me like doubloons in

5 •

BEGINNINGS (HOT SHITS)

the dark. Rock and roll meant grunge glamour, high times, reckless women, unwholesome joyous noise. I'd been in love with rock for almost a decade, though I'd never held a guitar or smacked a drum, only listened and wondered, listened and moved.

Pelops, it turned out, was a rock security guy. He was the head of front-gate security at Roosevelt Stadium, a sixty-thousand-seat showcase in Jersey City, New Jersey, that this summer, the summer of '74, would host all of the top touring acts: he mentioned the Grateful Dead, the Allman Brothers, Emerson, Lake & Palmer; maybe the Stones would show up.

But why was it such a big deal to be head of front-gate security? Pelops was ready for me on this. Because that's where all the action is: That's where the drugs are slung and the cops congregate to do their dirty business and the unwashed multitudes make their play for free admission. That's where the most beautiful honeys are to be seen first and maybe waylaid; that's the main transit point between the music and the world. And after you've done your job at the gate, you go backstage and you catch the show and you party with the rockers, if you choose. (Pelops made it clear that sometimes he chose not to, for some rockers were not up to his standards.) From the front gate, it seemed, you commanded the world. You could become what Pelops Kazanjian took himself to be, a King of Rock and Roll.

I knew that I was in trouble. I had a weakness then for people like Pelops Kazanjian, kings of rock and roll, or kings of this or that. I loved the types who, where I grew up, were commonly called hot shits. I loved people who took up the whole room, put on an act, sucked all the oxygen out of the atmosphere and sent it back to you as intoxicating ether. I loved big talkers, bullshitters, kingly clowns. I found these people and I followed them around. I marveled at their indestructibility. I reveled at how ready they seemed to jump back to life from every ass whipping they sustained.

I was at a point of crossing in my life then—a liminal moment, as the anthropologists like to say. I was trying to figure out what the world was about and what my place in it was going to be. And somehow I got the idea that these characters, these kings, could help me along. They were figures out of quest romance—I'd studied those in lit class, yes I had—and their function, like that of the wise men and monarchs and white witches in Spenser's *Faerie Queene* and the Arthurian tales, might be to set me on my path. For I thought of myself as something of a quester, perhaps not altogether unlike any young man or woman setting off into the world. As I liked to put it to myself, keeping matters aptly vague so as to allow for the ministrations of good fortune in all forms, I was looking for *it*.

What was *it*? I did not know for certain. I had no concrete vision of *it*s ultimate form. That was part of the beauty. *It* was the thing in life that I was tooled for and set to do and to be: it was the way of living in the world that would give me spiritual and intellectual and—who knows?—maybe erotic satisfaction, too. I had an idea that there was a right path for me out there, but that it was not going to be an easy thing to find. I remember being both inspired and daunted by a line of Emerson's from "Self-Reliance." Speaking of—and to—a young person coming out into the world, the Concord Sage says, "The power which resides in him is new in nature, and none but he knows what that is that he can do, nor does he know until he has tried." It was a matter of finding out

7   •

what that thing was, or failing in the quest—which would be failing in life.

Pelops was the first of the kings who took the time to stop and point my way, but he was far from the only one. (When you go looking for these characters, you'll find that they're not in short supply.) They led me, and I led myself, into some strange places in my search for this odd, elusive Grail, this *it*. I sought the thing in the sacred sites, or at least in those counted sacred at the time: in drugs and sex and politics and wealth and poverty and in movies and in books. The quest took me into the rock business, into a stretch driving a cab in Manhattan, to too many all-day and late-night movie theaters, to a gig at a discotheque (I still can't hear KC and the Sunshine Band without shaking with internal woe), out (way out) into nature, and at last into a job teaching at a strange and wonderful hippie school—maybe the last hippie school in America, I'm not sure.

I found *it*, too, or at least I think I did. But by that point my whole sense of *it*, the holy unholy thing, had changed, and I had changed as well. As T. S. Eliot says, in language that's beautiful, to be sure, but maybe a little exalted to fit my situation, "the purpose is beyond the end you figured / And is altered in fulfillment." And *it*—or at least my version—has now passed away, at least for me.

For the last twenty-five years, I've been a college teacher, accustomed to seeing my students grasp their diplomas and step out into the world, not always as subtly and strongly equipped as I'd like. The years following graduation are as tough as any I've encountered (though I expect that they are as nothing compared to old age): so here's a graduation gift, for better and for worse, made of paper, and a little more. I've told some stories and—unwilling and probably unable to shuck the teacherly part of my soul—have leaned an arm against the mantelpiece and reflected a little on those stories, too.

In these pages, I've done the things that memoirists now are compelled to do: changed all names (except the ones that belong to well-known figures), modified a few personal descriptions, merged a couple of minor characters—worked, in short, to keep privacy intact. Where controlled substances are concerned—and you can't write about the time without treating them—I've added not one layer of gauze but two or three. In one case, I modified a time sequence to make the narrative flow a little more smoothly. The lines in quotes are as I recall them, but they can't possibly be right word for word. Ultimately this is my truth, the way it was for me.

But up ahead I see Pelops Kazanjian striding across the Bennington campus, forced-marching into the future. I hear his voice, too. "Enough with the bourgeois apologetics, Edmundson! What are you going to do? You only have another month in this fool's paradise, and then what? You have no idea. But you want the world, don't you? You want everything! I can tell!"

It's true, what he's saying. I begin to run after him. I can't help it. "Wait up, Pelops. Wait up!"

THE KING OF ROCK AND ROLL

(music)

"Is that a scaling ladder that they've got there?" I asked Pelops. We were standing in front of Roosevelt Stadium, the sixty-thousand-seater that he had told me all about that morning at Bennington. Technically speaking, the fact that a bunch of kids—fifteen, sixteen, seventeen years old; there looked to be about fifty of them—had built a ladder for scaling the lowest wall of the stadium and getting into the show, en masse, without paying, wasn't my business. I was on the stage crew by then, the working aristocracy of the Schneider-Hamlin Production Company. But Pelops, who as front-gate security boss for tonight's Pink Floyd show should have been concerned, was now my roommate and my closest New York friend. I had to let him know what was up.

A week after our forced march across the Bennington

College campus, Pelops popped the question. He called me at Bennington during Sunday coffee hour. Graduation was only two weeks away, and I still had no idea what I was going to do. Would I like to come to New York? Would I take a job in rock and roll?

At the front gate of the stadium, where I was vainly trying to get Pelops's attention, people were screaming and yelling; occasional fights were boiling up; a Jersey City policeman had threatened—facetiously, I imagined—to crack my skull with his baton. But I was exactly where I wanted to be in the world and having a fine, fine time. I'd been in love with rock and roll for quite a while. Not long ago, rock and roll had sprung me, opened new worlds. Maybe rock could do it for me one more time.

When Pelops made the offer, I jumped. The gang sipping tea and crumbling cookies in the Bennington dorm living room heard me yelp like a Texas cowboy. My dreams were coming at me. Why not say it? In some part of my soul, I wanted to be a writer/magician/visionary/fortune-and-misfortune teller. I wanted to get a hand on the Zeitgeist's rump. Maybe both hands, maybe ride. My fellow grads were going to trot off to law school and publishing houses and PhD programs in Comp Lit and Modern Studies and, my college, Bennington, being what it was, to pristinely disordered lofts in SoHo and vacant family apartments in Paris and London. But when I signed on with Pelops that night at Bennington, I was sure that I was putting myself at the center of the world's churning gyre.

I eventually moved in with Pelops and Dave, the production company's stage manager, in a scuzz-afflicted three-story walk-up in Washington Heights. I worked security at the beginning, under Pelops's dubious tutelage, and then got promoted to the stage crew. I did the Grateful Dead; the Allman Brothers; Emerson, Lake & Palmer ("Welcome back my friends to the show that never ends"—then the organ music climbs the stairs); Alice Cooper; Eric Clapton; and others of comparable standing and style.

It was 1974 when I started working at rock shows; the sixties were in their fourteenth year, and the party was continuing. The draft was over; the Vietnam War was well and truly lost; the porcine Agnew had been convicted and sent packing; and though the anti-Messiah in the White House hadn't yet resigned, the Watergate prosecutors were on him like hounds. He had only a few weeks left. I was sure that my job at rock would be another installment in the grand celebration of the victory of the young, the cool, and the semi- to seismically stoned. And given my past history with the music, I had a hunch that the job might add up to more. Here I might find the thing I was vaguely, aimlessly questing after.

Pelops seemed supremely indifferent to what I was telling him about the scaling ladder and the fifty or so kids about to begin a medieval-style assault on the Pink Floyd show. He was staring off toward the horizon, thinking his elevated thoughts. Finally he looked at me with genial exasperation. "What *is* this about?" he said. "Is it about workers? Is it about peasants? Is it about the impending overthrow of the international bourgeoisie?"

Pelops was a self-celebrating Marxist. He'd mastered all the major texts and many of the minor installments, too. He rumbled down the street, quoting at top volume from Lenin's denunciation of the "renegade Kautsky." He had a many-megaton IQ. At NYU, his father was a mainstay of the art history faculty with a thick row of the forbidding books that he'd written lined up over his desk; he called it his vanity shelf. Pelops didn't look to be grad-school material; he was the revolution on crank.

Both of Pelops's parents were diminutive. Where did they get Pelops?—he with his swag belly and the vast nose turned up, the nostrils looking like infernal tunnels. Pelops stared hard at the world with those tiny eyes that seemed determined to burn through whatever he looked on. I'm surprised those X-ray peepers didn't draw smoke from their objects. What did Pelops see with his laser eyes? He saw bourgeois affectation. He saw reactionary jive. That's what rock and roll and most of the other cultural sideshows around were for Pelops—dancing bubbles on top of capitalism's evil brew, made of human blood and broken human bones and groaning sinews.

As the kids began to scale the wall, Pelops finally took them in. He was no doubt trying to decide whether he actually gave enough of a damn to do anything. Pelops had his commitments to the workers and the peasants, sure, but it sometimes seemed that his chief allegiance was to trouble. Pelops liked explosions, mishaps, disorder. Probably he was wondering whether letting the kids bust in and then trying to run them down inside the stadium would provide more diversion than going after them on the outside. Or maybe he was simply standing here doing his mental calisthenics, recalling six or so choice pages from *Das Kapital*, volume 2, making sure that he still had them down verbatim.

"That's good," he finally said with cinematic weariness, "that's fairly good. Last week they actually used a battering ram. They blew through the south gate." Then he told a few of his guys to go over to the ladder and put an end to things.

The four security guys flew up in close formation and pushed into the crowd like a blade; soon they were at the ladder and shaking it, shaking it, though not yet full force. A few kids were on the top, just about to get on the wall. They were sixteen, maybe twenty feet in the air. Were the kids going to come down voluntarily? There was some spirited back-and-forth about this. But finally yes, luckily, they did. The security guys might actually have been willing to shake the kids down to the ground, like young green apples from a tree.

It was only the late afternoon of Pink Floyd, and before the evening disappeared, there would be numberless fistfights, bad trips, general mayhem, needless battles, unnecessary blood-letting. Granted, this was Pink Floyd, which didn't bring out the opera crowd. The Grateful Dead were perhaps more di-verting. They came with the Hells Angels, who were sup-posedly there to provide security. Before that show, Pelops offered me a paternal warning: Stay away from the Angels. When they come onto the scene, amble off. They have one law in regard to disputes with outsiders, "One on all, all on one." If you get into trouble with one of them, no matter how wrong he might be, they'll converge and they'll do you in. It happened to Hunter Thompson, Pelops said; it can happen to you. But I was not always in the mood to take paternal advice from Pelops. I needed to discover things on my own.

After a certain point at the Dead show, everyone who worked for the production company came backstage, Pelops included. The crowd was so crazed on moldy acid that there was no securing the stadium at large. People simply had at each other. Angels and security guys and even the stage crew guarded the elevated stage and the backstage area. From time to time, the crowd made a run for this part of the fort or that, and the security guys and the Angels fended them off with predictable methods.

I ended up on the far left edge of the perimeter beside an Angel with a Pappy Yokum beard and a tattered brown slouch hat on his head. He said his name was Squeegee, or something like that. Squeegee was immersed in an amphetamine rap, akin probably to the ones that the famous Dean Moriarty used to deliver in the garage where Ken Kesey and the Merry Pranksters were tuning up the Bus. Squeegee was doing speed-freak variations on a theme, and the theme was his need to kill his old lady as soon as possible. She'd been messing around on him, or so he claimed. I, the budding moralist, suggested to Squeegee—with whom I'd already had a pleasant talk on whether or not the Dead would play more of what he wanted, which was "shit-kickin' music"—that killing his old lady might be a bad idea. Umbrage, enormous and immediate umbrage, was taken. Pelops hadn't told me, but I might have known that after they've been offended, Angels find all explanations hopelessly pedantic. Squeegee heated up.

Out of the corner of my eye, I saw two other Angels striding over to participate in the seminar. One of them was a man-mountain, Pelops-size, maybe larger. I noticed that in a blunt-fingered paw he was holding a vessel about the size of a twelve-ounce Budweiser bottle, the same dark brown color with the slight gold tinge, but obviously not a Bud bottle. The man-mountain screwed the cap off the container and pushed it under Squeegee's nose. His eyes opened very wide, his ears seemed to climb the side of his head. His scalp, or what I saw of it beneath the mountain-man hat, looked to be rising. Then he closed his eyes tight, as though he were trying to compress his whole skull. He took the bottle from his nose, gave the man-mountain a look of intense gratitude, and passed it to the third Angel.

When it was my turn, I put the bottle under my nostrils and gave it a mild sniff. Did Emily Dickinson say that she knew she was reading a real poem when she felt like the top of her head was coming off? My whole head felt like it was coming off. My brain became a blast furnace. Blood flowed up in geysers, and soon I heard an intense rushing noise as though Niagara Falls was inside my cranium and all the blood that had shot up was now running down in torrents. Squeegee looked at me with benevolence. The slate of his mind had been wiped clean.

A few minutes later, Pelops came by and I told him the story of my miraculous rescue. "What the hell was that stuff?" I asked him. "Jesus, Edmundson, do you know nothing? That was amyl nitrite; they use it to restart people's hearts when they've stopped." (I was sure that it could do that and more.) I expressed interest in a deeper acquaintance with this substance. Pelops informed me that nothing killed brain cells like amyl nitrite and that even he would never touch the stuff. "What about the Angels? What about their brain cells?" I asked. They were twenty yards away, still hitting off the bottle. Pelops began laughing and couldn't stop.

At rock and roll, Pelops was grand: He strode around the front gate with a length of pipe in one hand and a bullhorn in the other. He bellowed at his crew; he bellowed at the concertgoers; he bellowed at the Jersey City cops, who bellowed back. He jumped into every front-gate confrontation, and there were plenty of them. He let his friends in for nothing, and when the promoter complained, Pelops denounced him as a bloated lackey of the capitalist musicmongers. The promoter might have answered that that's more or less what Pelops was, too. Surely he was big enough, weighing something near three bills. And standing at the front gate, he was also the guy who kept the Garden State Summer Music Festival, as it was absurdly called, from turning into Woodstock. He made sure there was no free concert. Whether anyone should pay for music was a big political issue at the time. All rock, some said, should belong to the people (along with all power). The only concert worth the name was a free concert. Ask Pelops about his role in stanching people's culture, though, and you were in for a lecture on the Marxist-Hegelian concept of "contradiction." This sort of contradiction was different from other sorts, in that a Marx-Hegel contradiction indicated that we were on the cusp of political change. It wasn't easy to talk your way around Pelops Kazanjian.

By and large, Pelops had only contempt for rock music. He denounced it constantly. He hung around for the mind bending and the mayhem, but about the music, he gave not a shit. The whole thing was tricks and toys. Woodstock Nation was all over, and it had never existed to begin with. This attitude of Pelops's was maybe to be expected. But the strange thing was that virtually everyone else who worked security or stage crew was as apparently closed down to the music as he was.

Every job—vocation, avocation, or pickup—has its protocols, including its unwritten rules of demeanor. French shopgirls pout with lips carefully puffed this far but no farther; the operator of the carnival ride has his proper dismal slouch;

bankers unbutton their vest's bottom button—or they do not. I was blown away to find that the demeanor for rock workers on security and on the stage crew was cool bordering on comatose. There seemed to be a rule in place: one must not, under any circumstances, respond to the music. So the security guards on the perimeter of the backstage area stood stiff as London grenadiers, while a few feet away bopped and jived the multitudes. You had to be indifferent to the music. Earplugs, no matter who was playing, were a sign of belonging, like the green schoolboy book bags they used to affect in the Harvard English Department or the beret worn at a certain prescribed angle in certain departments at the University of Chicago.

I was mystified. My own affair with rock and roll had taken a while to get going, but when it did, it changed everything. When I was in the sixth grade, I told my mother with real chagrin that I seemed to be the only kid in my class who couldn't connect with the Beatles. I had become something of a Beethoven admirer thanks to my father, who played the symphonies at sky-splitting volume on Sunday mornings. (You half expected to see Zeus come ripping out of the clouds.) The Beethoven was probably my father's idea of a religious observance: he never went to church. In school, I came on strong on Beethoven's behalf. This, along with my thick glasses and substantial nose (which my father eventually taught me to call Roman), put me in the invisible but virtually escape-proof dungeon of the uncool.

But then the Rolling Stones came along, and oddly enough, they were my sort of thing. They were crude, hard-driving, hungry, untaught and proud to be. It turned out that I was some of these things, too. Beethoven and the Stones have more in common, maybe, than the Stones and the Beatles. The Stones and Beethoven seem to heartily wish for one thing, and that is to take no shit. I must have played *Aftermath* four hundred times.

The Stones were on my side! They hated school, teachers, the well-taught, the slick, and they hated—or at least they were righteously contemptuous of—the great jeweled enigma of my life, girls. The Stones knew that Eros was warfare by another name; that guys came pathetically underprepared for the struggle; that the other side had constant advantage. "Under My Thumb," where the guy actually is on top, running the show, is about a rare reversal. ("She's the sweetest . . . pet in the world!") We—with our silly-sad stick-up needs and the subtler need of replacing the mother-love that we were so energetically repudiating—were under *their* thumbs. Couldn't anybody see? The Beatles were the girls' band. She loves you and *you know* that can't be bad: Do what she says, capitulate. Hold her hand.

Being a Stones lover was about being willing to piss anywhere. And on anything. The Stones were defiant, crude, hungry kids out of the working class—who didn't want to work. ("Never want to be like poppa, workin' for the boss every night and day.") When I mouthed off to a teacher, which I did plenty, Keith's tomcat chords and Mick's yowl were in the background (heard only by me).

The Stones were the piss-anywhere band. Piss anywhere: you had a dick, and you were proud of it. Girls and women, with their erotic magic, ruled the world, but there was one thing they could not do, one act they couldn't perform. Only we could piss standing up—anywhere. So piss where you like: the world was no way yours, but you marked territory still, because you had more bristle and bite than the deeded owners. Piss where you please: convention, cleanliness, and their near neighbor, godliness, had all frozen icy white, and they needed a warm dose of yellow contempt to thaw them out. The world was your urinal. Your high-arc whiz was the signature of exultation, back-alley transcendence. Drilling it at the ground was at some point bound to start a seismic crack in the crust of the earth. Piss promiscuously—Mick did, Keith did. Charlie and Bill watched their backs.

I loved the Animals, too. (What were we all—girls included, maybe—but animals?) I loved their simple, bluesy rhythms—the faith they had in the basic form of their music, Mississippi Delta stuff fed through a Fender amp. But the Animals were too much about complaint and contrition. They were the bad boys who broke down and blubbered in the principal's office. "O lord, *please* don't let me be misunderstood." "We gotta get out of this place." (Life's so, so hard.) The Stones were contempt and no contrition. They never cried for mercy, never said that they'd had enough; they'd never whine with regret about how they or their daddies had misbehaved in the House of the Rising Sun. As long as somebody had another couple of quid for pints all around, the party reeled on.

So what could I do when Abbie Hoffman went after the Stones the way that he did? In my senior year of high school, Abbie was a demigod to me. He was the author of *Revolution for the Hell of It*, an instigator of the Youth International Party (the Yippies), who threw dollars down onto the blind mouths working the floor of the New York Stock Exchange. His voice, as I felt it rise off the page, made the sound of pleasantly shearing metal. It played havoc with the doldrum hum of the family TV on the other side of my bedroom door. "*McHale's Navy*'s on. Wanna watch *McHale's Navy*?"

It wasn't precisely the Stones that Abbie cut loose on, but it might as well have been. It was the Who, the British band that at the time, 1970, had similar clout. Abbie railed at the Who for flying into Woodstock in a helicopter, chomping steak, sucking champagne, staying aloof from the crowd, and demanding big bucks. When their set was over, they didn't join Woodstock Nation in the mud. Roger Daltrey didn't merge his immortal voice in the immortal "No Rain!" chant. Pete Townsend didn't get naked and soap up in the communal pool. No, they acted like . . . they acted like celebrities. They acted like rock stars. They came in and reproduced the culture of entertainment glitz that the spirit of Woodstock should have made obsolete.

I gave Abbie's book a ride. I sent it into a clumsy bird flight against my poster of drunk and disordered Hells Angels. It hit with a splat. I was surprised not to see dead-bird entrails bulging out of it. The Stones, the Who—these were my liberating gods. They were free in themselves, and they made other people free.

What were the liberating gods prophesying? What inspiration came from their Boone's Farm– or Ripple– or (God save us) Dom Perignon–anointed lips? They dramatized many hopes, gave shape to many visions. The Beatles, in the phase of theirs that I liked the best, were the road to a lovely lotus world: Blake would have called it Beulah, the place where there's no struggle or strife, and all contraries are equally true. That's the world of Lucy in the Sky with her Diamonds, of the Yellow Submarine. It's Pepperland, once it's been washed clean of Blue Meanies, and it's the Strawberry Fields that go on and on and on Forever. What an amazing piece of good luck it was to grow up with the Beatles, as my contemporaries and I did, almost exactly. They were kids like us in 1963, when they first came to America—singing impossibly catchy songs (albeit girls' songs) about the joys and dramas of the high-school dance: "Twist and Shout," "I Saw Her Standing There," "She Loves You." Then for the next six years, they stayed out ahead of us, breaking new paths, getting into mysticism and drugs and every form of musical expression, from the sitar and highly spiritualized Indian music to Tin Pan Alley, British music hall stuff. They started out as tough Liverpool kids, interested in not much more than the mundane, exuberant pleasures of the corner, the dance hall, and the pub, and made themselves into seers, ready to take you on the Magical Mystery Tour and to tell you that, if you'd followed them on the trip, all you needed—truly—was love. By the time they'd broken up and John was chanting "The Ballad of John and Yoko," they'd compressed a lifetime of creation—followed by fierce disillusionment—into a small, small space of years. How did they move so fast? Why ever did they quit and leave us behind?

The Grateful Dead were a weed-blown collective meandering through the realms of soft sound and soft light. The Beach Boys were cruisers: in their cars, on their boards, in their slidingly mellifluous vocals, they rode the surface of life, skimming its tough-looking waves, never getting dumped, rarely even wet. Joni Mitchell's music was the song of the soul in love—wounded, astray, sometimes self-misunderstanding, and always misunderstood, but uncompromising in its feeling that love, head over heels, was the only worthwhile state to be in. Love let you see more; it made you kinder and crazier, too. Joni scrambled your sense of proportion. "I could drink a case of you and still be on my feet": Is that the worst lyric line ever written or one of the best? Is it crazy love, erotomania? Or is it life's one true holy condition? And the Stones, my unwashed gods? They rambled here and there, rulers of the world: zipping up in the alley after putting a piss fresco on the wall, a hundred dollars in each guy's pocket—gotta spend it all tonight.

To me, the high-school kid, the rockers said many things, but all of rock said one thing, too. And that thing was simple: wake up! Every rock song worth anything holds it as a matter of faith that we're asleep—numb, comatose, dead—in the inner and the outer life. What Coleridge liked to call Life in Death is the standard human condition. (Coleridge, grieving, looks out on a stunning landscape full of marvels that cannot touch him at all: "I see them all so excellently fair. / I see, not feel, how beautiful they are!") Our desires have gone cold. We've got nothing to look forward to. Without knowing it, we've given up the ghost.

But as the song goes, "Don't bury me 'cause I ain't dead yet." Rock has a primal scene. The kids are all bunched snug and sad at their school desks, living in sardine world. The teacher is droning on like a factory machine, the kind that the kids will soon be running, nine to five, nine to five, nine to five. The ceilings are low, the windows are sooty, the radiators are chugging—the schoolroom, which is also an office, a factory, a loading dock, a jail, a barracks, has become a crypt. When from outside the door comes the ripping noise of a power chord. It's an *electric* guitar: music has dueled with the machine, has won, and now the machine sounds brassy, lovely, and pissed. It's the life knell that's sounding, not the death. The guitar tolls for everybody. It tolls for thee. In a hyperelegant slide, like butter across a hot smooth griddle, knees to the floor, pants so tight they look sprayed on, jacket cut blade-sharp, comes Elvis or Buddy Holly or Bo Diddley or, knees willing, Eric Clapton. He sends his right arm up in a windmill arc, and before it comes across the face of the guitar like the hand of hyperaccelerated time, the kids are up and the kids are moving. Rock and roll forever! Gonna die before I get old, and I ain't never, never gonna die. What we have here is a religious moment: it's electric Jesus coming on with his body and blood, rock-and-roll wine and rock-and-roll bread.

Rock to me then was pagan resurrection, rebirth in the body for joy and kicks everlasting. We were all dead most of the time (even between songs) because almost everything that wasn't rock was a killer. Rock then was just what the witch doctor ordered for the thing that plagued us all in the post-industrial consumer collective: boredom—along with boredom's counterpart (or maybe it's boredom's deep content), what the White Negro called "muted, icy, self-destroying rage." We eat too much shit. We smolder when we ought to burn, dissect life rather than living it. Rock is king because it gets all the buried energies up and flowing free, calling to us like Jesus (Yes!) at the gate of Lazarus's tomb.

So what was up at Roosevelt Stadium, only a couple years after I'd left high school and rock satori? At least a few of the three hundred or so people who staffed the shows must have liked some of the bands. I surely did. The prospect of being on the scene and hearing the best music in the world, live, was what had me so jazzed, what made me yelp when Pelops popped the question during that Bennington coffee hour. When we were at the stadium, after setting up, hanging out, it was all about the party. Everybody drank Green Boys, as we called Heinekens; some sucked jays; some laid down lines.

But let the band play a chord, and the staff became a mélange of funeral directors. They were protozombies. They seemed to be playing the role of rock's number-one enemies. I don't mean the buttoned-up schoolteacher or the minister wearing his hair shirt. They're standard-issue straight men; they're easy marks. I mean the young, ostensibly hip and open, who, invited to the resurrection, prefer to stay dead. It's as though Lazarus told Jesus to bugger off—no miracles wanted today, thanks. I'll stay here inside the stone igloo.

Was it because the guys at rock were only the grease inside rock's glorious machine? Were they expressing what Georg Lukacs—assuming he'd abdicated his spot at some Marxist think tank in Hungary and come cruising through Jersey past the stadium in a blue Cadillac, drinking Budweisers and catcalling honeys—were they expressing what Lukacs would have wanted them to call class consciousness? Pelops got bounced from his job once because he sat at the front door of the Capitol Theater, the production company's winter venue, supposedly guarding the gate, reading Lenin's *What Is to Be Done?* "If I'd been reading *Luscious Lesbians of Venus*, I'd still have a job," Pelops proclaimed.

I wasn't immediately convinced by Pelops's political analysis of rock, though I couldn't dismiss it out of hand, either. Abbie, you could see, wanted to be onstage with the Who; if they'd have given him a microphone and let him sing, he would have dropped all charges. But Pelops, for all his lassitude and babe chasing (actually, women loved Pelops—he was hyperovert; he made no bones, and this was somehow appealing), did care about the wretched of the earth. To Pelops, rock was a job. He could watch the last spasms of a desperate empire, throwing a party to keep the great suffering mass at bay. At rock Pelops launched many, many denunciations about the kids cavorting at the Masque of the Red Death. Still, he never missed a show. As he liked to say, "Whenever you go out to Jersey, something you can't possibly believe will happen does." At times, he referred to himself as the King of Rock and Roll—the phrase porcupinelike, sharp-quilled everywhere with irony.

During the time I knew Pelops, he was thrown off his game only once. This occurred around Christmas. Pelops was involved with a young woman whose mother was a figure in the New York literary world. Not surprisingly, she had qualms about her dear and only daughter spending time with a genius, rock-and-roll, Marxist semi-thug, and she often put her reservations on record, aloud and in writing. But Christmastime came, and one afternoon, the spirit of Scrooge redeemed rose up, or if you listened to Pelops, the spirit was called up through the medium of a few unscheduled whiskey and sodas. The phone rang and the estimable mother, sailing all over the harbor, many sheets to the wind, invited Pelops— "It is time we got to know and appreciate each other, things being what they are"—to her literary magazine's holiday extravaganza, such as that was.

The flower of New York lit culture was in attendance. Pelops showed up wearing his rock-and-roll blue jeans stained with crankcase oil and his plaid shirt—a major concession: it was the only non-T-shirt he possessed and the first time that he'd worn it in a year. He clumped himself down in a corner of the party, removed from his pocket a couple of dozen diminutive, tightly rolled pieces of business, laid them out like machine-gun ammo, put the first in his mouth, ignited it, and went to work. He had warned his hostess about this. He had told her that the only way that he could manage a party would be by keeping something burning all the time. So he sat like Buddha and puffed like a bomb factory.

There were worried conversations, whisperings, noddings, shushings. How do we deal? Is this character likely to go crazy and obliterate the room? What is to be done? The hostess entered consultation with her best friend in attendance, the much-esteemed Susan Sontag. Sontag—author of brilliant essays and semireadable novels; brave, gifted, trouble-creating woman of letters; about six feet tall, with the regal face of Jewish Athena and a white stripe (Agape) running through her raven-colored hair (Eros)—signed on as the one-woman SWAT team. She marched across the room and stood over Pelops for a moment, looking down at him as though from the mountaintop. Then, with an estimable lack of grace, she flopped onto the floor, put a long forefinger on his blue-jeaned, oil-stained knee, and said, "Hi, I'm Susan. What's your sign?"

"Aquarius," Pelops admitted. Pelops was an Aquarian: a walking harbinger of the new age.

"Pelops, I believe you were taken aback," I said to him, when he told me the story.

"Indeed," he said. "For a while I couldn't get a word out. But then we talked about astrology. She was actually a fairly good shit." From Pelops, no higher compliment was likely to come, unless it was a matter of revolutionary credentials.

At the Pink Floyd show, I must have strolled out to visit Pelops a half dozen times. For the sake of entertainment and edification, I often went out and consorted with him when the stage crew took a break, and sometimes when it didn't. I had (and have) a dose of what my fellow Irishman Oscar Wilde called the indolence of our race. But at Pink Floyd, I had the right to a little goldbricking. I'd earned it.

Pink had demanded a certain quality of sound. They wanted their amps stacked high, not just onstage, so they were so broad and high and forbidding that they looked like a barricade at the Paris Commune. They also wanted amp clusters at three points around the stadium, three highly elevated points. I spent the morning of the show channeling the spirits of the pyramid builders, humping the huge blocks of wood and circuitry up and up and up the stairs of the decayed old bowl. From the top of the stadium, the bowl's lip, I looked not on the Sahara, with Bedouin on camelback making their slo-mo way across the dunes, which I had every reason to expect, but on ruined Jersey City, spread out like a bombed metropolis from the European theater of the War.

Out there somewhere in the noble American trash heap, there lived the gangbangers with whom I'd done some negotiation when I was Pelops's associate chief at the front gate. The stadium was on their turf, they said, and they threatened to torch the place and everyone in it if they didn't get free admission to the Crosby, Stills, Nash & Young show, in which—they were a Hispanic gang—none of them seemed to have the least interest. I got in between the gang boss and three or four screaming security guys, took the gang around to a side entrance, and let them all in. Twenty minutes later, they began throwing concrete chunks down in the direction of the security guys who had disrespected them, having first warned me, their new pal, to step aside and under the metal awning, *por favor.* "Ha, ha," the boss called down to me, "they *maricón*s, but you alright." When Pelops heard about it, he claimed that I should have gone into single combat, mano a mano, with one of them, to the death presumably, to decide if they'd come in or not. From the promoter's point of view, I would have been the Neville Chamberlain of rock security. But Pelops never told. I'd have been fired, and Pelops needed me there to observe him, remember his exploits, and record them for posterity.

The night of Crosby, Stills, Nash & Young, the night of the near-rumble with the street gang, was a big night for another reason. It was the night that Richard Milhous Nixon resigned. The band made the announcement and kicked into "Long Time Gone." Fireworks tore through the air, and blue dragons of smoke coiled and rose around the stage. The crowd went mad. We'd won. We'd taken it. The revolution had come to a climax, and the forces of change, hope, and Panama Red had had their way. Now we could get ready for a new heaven and a new earth. Pelops was about the only one I saw not doing an improvised version of the boogaloo as soon as the news came down. He stood backstage, arms crossed over his huge chest, looking in exasperation up toward the sky, hoping, maybe, that someone would have the where-withal to photograph or film or at least recollect the one guy in the crowd who sensed that what looked like a victory for peace and love and all the rest was really nothing of the kind. Meet the new boss; same as the old boss.

Before my extended break with Pelops late on the after-noon of the Pink Floyd show, we'd installed the sound altars at the acoustically most desirable parts of the stadium, and we'd finished another assignment, too. We'd put the parachutelike white silken roof that Pink required over the stage. It took about six hours to get the thing up and in position. We were told that this was the first use of the roof, and Pink's guys were unsteady. They had some blueprints, but those turned out not to be much good. Eventually the roof did rise and inflate, with American know-how applied. The know-how involved a lot of spontaneous knot-tying and strategic guy-rope tangling. Pink's roadies were all Brits, experts at talking about things. Even I felt mechanically adept next to them.

Pink went on at about ten o'clock that night, and the sound altars that we'd built, expending all that servile sweat, didn't work. People sat on them or kicked them or cut the cords—big surprise for Jersey City. From the stage, you could see the amp towers rise up in silhouette, looking like overbuilt pagan grave markers there along the top of the stadium wall. Pink made its noise, the towers stayed mute, the mob lit its lighters at the end (the first time we'd seen this, I think), and we spent three hours breaking the amps down and loading the truck. We refused to go after the ones up the stadium steps, and after some sharp words, Pink's guys had to scramble up and retrieve them.

There was almost always tension between the roadies and the stage crew. One time, at a show by (if memory serves) Queen, their five game roadies got into a brawl with a dozen of our stage-crew guys; then the house security, mostly Jersey bikers and black karate devotees, heard the noise and jumped in. Queen's roadies held on for a while, but finally they saw it was a lost cause. One of them grabbed a case of champagne from the truck cab and opened a bottle and passed it—all became drunk and happy.

Pink's road manager wanted the inflatable roof brought gently down, folded, and packed securely in its wooden boxes. The problem was that the thing was full of helium and no one knew where the out-valve was; also, we'd secured it to the stage with knots that would've given the Marquis de Sade pause. Everyone was tired. Those who were once stoned were no longer. It was about four o'clock in the morning and time to go home. An hour went into concocting strategies to get the floating pillowy roof down. It became a regular seminar. Then Frank—Franko—Bell stepped in. He was a round, strong, blond-haired guy, our crew chief, who looked like a good-natured Hessian captain, who loved laughing and cake, and who defended the integrity of his stage crew at every turn, even going so far as to have screamed back at Stevie Nicks, who was screaming at me for having dropped a guitar case, telling her that he was the only one who has the right to holler at Edmundson, thus bringing over into the fray other members of Fleetwood Mac, also dispatched by Franko. Much more could be said to distinguish Franko from the average run of crew chiefs and mere mortals, but maybe it's enough to say that faced by the Pink Floyd roof crisis, Franko did what he always could be counted on to do in critical circumstances, which is to say, he did something.

Franko walked softly to a corner of the stage, reached into his pocket, removed a buck knife, and with it began to saw one of the ropes attaching the holy celestial roof to the stage. Three or four of us, his minions, did the same. "Hey, what are you doing?" wailed Pink's head roadie. "I'll smash your—" Then it became clear that Franko had a knife in his hand and that some of the rest of us did, too. In the space of a few minutes, we sawed through the ropes. There came a great sighing noise as the last thick cord broke apart. For a moment, there was nothing; for another moment, more of the same. Then the roof, like a gorgeous cloud, white and soft, rose, rose dream-like as the sun burst out, red and raw, from the near side of New Jersey, traveling in from England and France, and before that from Poland and Rumania and Persia and Xanadu and all the rest. The sunlight kissed the floating roof, giving it a soft crimson tinge, and making it look like a benevolent floating spacecraft, piloted by aliens beautiful, wise, and good. Franko started to laugh, a big beer-bellied, bear-bellied laugh. We all joined. Even Pink's guys did. We were like little kids on the last day of school. We were laughing like freed serfs, shaking loose chains together. We stood on the naked stage, watching the white craft go up and out, floating over the Atlantic, a gift from America back to the Old World. Some of us waved.

We'd had our rock-and-roll moment, at least for the day. It was quieter, much different than Buddy Holly, or whoever it was, sliding into class on his perfectly pegged pants, but it did what rock does: it woke us up—at least enough so we could drive home to New York and crash. But this moment was still a good-bye—a form of farewell.

"I get up," says Van Halen in what may be the rock-and-roll national anthem, "and nothing gets me down." Really? Well, I believe the part about getting up. Who can hear the organ intro to "Jump" without feeling a rush to the brain—free and legal coke? It's reveille time in resurrection city.

But what happens then? What do you do after rock has shaken you out of Life in Death?

Pick up your bed and walk—as the Savior told the man he brought back to his full powers.

OK, but where are you supposed to go?

Rock recharges the Will, as Schopenhauer, Lord of Pessimists, would have said. By the Will he means all of the appetites, the appetites for pleasure, power, sex, fun, freedom, what have you. But when the Will is recharged, what then?

Which of the appetites do you want to act on? Which should you act on?

Back in high school, the Stones helped get the dumb, coercive angels off my back; they aligned me with the forces of joyous insubordination. They sabotaged routine and all things routinized. But once the Stones and all the rest had knocked down the cell door, I wasn't at all sure which way I was supposed to run. What I responded to in rock was the rebel yell—but as to what the rebel was supposed to do on Monday morning, rock didn't have much to say, at least to me. Maybe there was a vision of fresh possibilities latent there: more art, more hanging out, more leisure, more sex, more music, more poetry, more friends—a nation of the young and hip inside the nation of the tired, repressive, and staid. But I never quite succeeded in finding a version of it all that fit me. And I suspect that some of my cohorts humping amps and guarding the gates may have felt the same way. Their indifference to the music was too aggressive, too pissed off, to be *merely* indifference. Maybe they were all living out a less articulate version of Pelops's critique of the music as another popcorn show, a scene of exploitation, appropriation, and all the rest. But maybe like me they had gravitated into the rock world because it once gave them something they valued—beautiful release—and they grew frustrated when it couldn't give them much of anything more.

In time, the advertising world, what some people think of as America's real popular culture, would make an amazing discovery about rock and roll—and the discovery is in line with what occurred to me and my buddies (maybe) there at the stadium. It's the jolt and the juice that matter most. The lyrics, the spirit, the vision, what have you—all have to take a backseat. Once the Will's activated by Keith's power chords and Mick's stray-cat *miaowwww*, it's possible to direct desire almost anywhere. The form, as they say in intro lit class, overwhelms the content. The backbeat, the flaming guitar licks, the playfully ominous organ do to the nervous system something like what steroids do to the muscles. But rock's effect is instantaneous. It hits home right away. It augments the energies, adds to the appetites—gives you more life. An electric guitar: that's what lightning would sound like, if you miked its indwelling spirit. Up from the stone slab, full of the storm's white energy, comes the new man. And what does this new man want, aside from another hit of rock?

It appears that he can want—or be made to want—almost anything. A blast of rock can put you in the mood to chuck the finger at the Combine and mess with Big Nurse. But it seems that it can also get you primed to buy a pair of sneakers, pick out a new car, or maybe survey some real estate on the Internet. Rock can be a prelude to a football game—the Stones often are. While "Start Me Up" ricochets off the stadium walls, U.S. Air Force jets flare overhead; on the field, the True-Faith Patriarchal Marching Band configures itself in the image of Old Glory. The sorcerer's apprentice, in the form of the young hip adman, is using the elixir of life to sell real estate and stocks and bonds, too.

It's no news that rock, which used to be entertaining subversion, in time became mere entertainment, if that. New bands come along and pretend to shake the old statues in the public square and give the ancestral gods a fright. But they're neglected or bought off or bought out. Makers of movie sound tracks squeeze the last pulp out of this ancient song or that, letting the oldsters get a final whiff of insurrection from the fragrant sounds. Motown hits from the sixties waft down the aisles at the organic grocery store.

But who was I to be ungrateful? Rock had done its thing for me once. It had been my flaming sword to swing against school and teachers and the boss. It had probably done as much to spring me out of my dismal high-school life as any other single force. A wise philosopher said that you can't step into the same stream twice, and maybe the man should have added that you can't expect even the most glorious angel to save you a second time either. In New York, I'd have a few more good moments with the music—including one that still shines for me like a sorcerer's ring. But ultimately rock wasn't the thing I was looking for. Becoming a player or a promoter or a deep, obsessive fan was a way for some people, maybe. But not for me. And though I kept my rock job the whole time I was in New York, it was clear that the music wasn't *it* for me. I had some more searching to do.

TAXI!

(money)

The rock-and-roll job didn't earn me much money, and the money that it did earn often ended up going to substances that made the job more bearable. There were times when it felt like I was working strictly to pay for what I required in order to work—coming from the background I did, I knew that this was not so uncommon a state. In my old neighborhood, it sometimes seemed that about 30 percent of the local dads' incomes went to beer, bourbon, and attendant snacks. I needed another way to put food—which in my case was frequently liver in its many forms, from calves' to beef to chicken to calves' again—onto the table. I settled on cab driving.

Pelops approved of this pursuit, believing it would deepen my connection with the proletariat. Yet he never seemed eager to acquire a hack license himself: he was happy to subsist on rock-and-roll money and occasional infusions from his generous parents. From time to time, Professor and Mrs.

Kazanjian even sent a cleaning woman up to 187th Street, knowing what they did about Pelops's sanitary habits and guessing what they did about mine. When I trudged off on a Thursday afternoon to hop the subway to Queens and get in line for a cab to take out for the night, Pelops frowned judiciously and nodded an approving nod but went back to his studies. Occasionally I dared to let Pelops know that I felt he was overdoing the theory part of Marxism and scanting the praxis, but this fazed him not at all. "I, Edmundson," he began, "am attempting to create myself as a vanguard intellectual and . . ." I knew that this sentence was only gaining traction for its five-mile looping journey through the dialectic, so out the door, Pelops-less, I went.

The city I stepped out into to ply my new trade was a mess. It was filthy, crime-filled, and corrupt. Soon it would be close to broke, and the rest of America would revel in its misery. The country at large wasn't doing so well, either. When Ford replaced Nixon in August 1974, expeditiously pardoning the archcrook, the *Times* announced that we were now faceup with "the worst inflation in the country's peacetime history, the highest interest rates in a century, [a] severe slump in housing, sinking and utterly demoralized security markets [whatever the hell a security market was], a stagnant economy with large-scale unemployment in prospect and a worsening international trade and payments position." Things only grew worse with time. Cabdrivers were constantly being robbed; occasionally one was murdered for the thirty-seven-odd dollars in his lockbox. (You could read about it on page twelve of the *Times*.) I wasn't in love with cab driving, but I needed money, so off into the infernal war of each against all I went.

My cab-driving buddy was a guy named Vince Duggan,

who, though only a freshman at Bennington the year I graduated, had already become famous at the college. Duggan was a tall, shambling guy who always seemed to be in a good mood. He was interested in everyone and charmed all, despite the fact that he had a bitter time remembering people's names. "I call a lot of people 'Tiny,'" he told me, and he did. As I walked across campus with this tall, charming shambler, he would call out to this person and that: "Hi, Tiny!" "Hey, Tiny, how you doing?" "Tiny, what's up?" There must have been something in the intonation. People loved him. Duggan also had a reputation for writing remarkable papers: he would hole up in the All Night Study, a room attached to the library, and there, puffing on Lucky Strikes and Chesterfields and whatever else he could bum, he turned out brilliant essays of prodigious length. In one, he compared the Homeric gods to players at a poker game: the comparison lasted twenty-five pages, and it held your interest—or at least it held mine.

Duggan lived on Park Avenue with his family, and he looked at cab driving as a major adventure. His love for the enterprise surpassed my understanding. Though he had a good job over the summer and during Bennington's winter break, editing at the *Village Voice*, he was always ready to sneak out of the editorial offices and make the trip to Queens, where we had to wait a minimum of two hours to get assigned our cabs. We needed to listen closely to hear our names called: The dispatchers studiously mispronounced every name that came up on their list. He was Du-GAN, accent on the second syllable; I was Ed-MUND-son, accent also on syllable two. What the dispatchers could do to a name like Mandirini or a Chalabala was a miracle to hear. Duggan was always game, always ready to go—for reasons that for a while escaped me, though I pieced them together soon enough. He was also, for an eighteen-year-old freshman paper-writing whiz, a pretty skilled cabbie.

Not me: from the beginning of my stint to the end, I was an amateur. This was true not only because my sense of direction was (and is) badly compromised, or because I had no idea how to get from Manhattan to Brooklyn or Queens, much less how to get back, or because I had a propensity for mixing up Grand Central Station and the Port Authority Terminal and frequently roared off toward one when the other was requested. No, there was also the fact that the whole cab-driving thing terrified me. Whenever I thought about what I was doing out there in my busted-up yellow chariot, I got the shakes. I feared that after my brief foray among the hiply well-to-do at Bennington, I was being tossed back in where I came from, with hardly a splash. I had again traded class identities, and this time, it might be for good. I started trying to work with the idea that I was destined to be a prole for life. It's not surprising that in my cab—with Pelops's approving specter looking on—I began developing something like class consciousness.

One night I picked up a party of four on Fifth Avenue and began to ferry them south. They were well dressed, prosperous, ready for a night on the town, their town. The host, the main man, sat beside me up front, and he commenced an oration: "Everyone says that London cabbies are the best in the world," he began. "They know the city like the backs of their hands, and all that. But for my money, New York cabbies are the best. They're by far the most interesting. And that's because a lot of them aren't professional cabbies at all. They're on the way to being something else. They're actors and writers and musicians. They aren't just hack drivers." His companions took this in, duly impressed.

The orator saw a visual aid ready to hand. "And look at this!" he trumpeted. "A book! New York cabbies read." He picked up my volume and turned it over so he could get a look at the cover. "*Selected Writings of Karl Marx*," he said, his voice dropping with each syllable. Then he fell into a silence that I found satisfying in the extreme.

I was reading about the revolution, plowing through the mountain range of texts that came to me from my swag-bellied visionary roommate. He offered continual tutelage on the classics of revolutionary invective but also on its more earthy forms. "Bourgeoisie, Bourgeoisie," he taught me to sing, to the tune of "Three Blind Mice": "See how they run. / See how they run. / When the revolution comes, / We'll kill them with knives and guns. / Bourgeoisie! Bourgeoisie!" On his T-shirt, Pelops wore many buttons, including one that commanded all perceivers to "Eat the Rich!" I asked him once how the rich tasted. "Not good. Not good at all, Ed-mundson." (Pelops, to be fair, was given to Chinese food and had a hard time mustering a positive word about much else.) "They're gamy and tough, and their fat smells of soap. But we have our duty, do we not?"

Under Pelops's bloodshot eyes, I read and reread the classics of dialectical materialism. They were piled high in his linoleum-floored bedroom, in precarious, ceiling-scraper stacks surrounding his mattress. When Pelops lay on his bed, he looked to be in a sort of prison. I was welcome to come in any time; I was welcome to take what I wanted. Really, I preferred novels and volumes of poetry, but Pelops refused to acquire those or to bring them uptown packed away in his

41 •

CHAPTER 2 : TAXI! (MONEY)

Russian-front coat, a great brown-bear covering on which he wore a snatch of red ribbon and a piece of brass—Order of Lenin, Fourth Class, I think it was.

Did I finish *Das Kapital*? It nearly finished me. I read it along with the works of Lenin and Mao and Fidel and Che. I even read Stalin's book on linguistics, which is better than anyone could hope. (The only good thing about Hitler's *Mein Kampf* is how awful it is.) Downstairs, Dave watched TV, read the *New York Post* and the *Times* from front to back, and worked his red telephone, laying plans for the arrival of the rock groups he stage-managed in New York and Jersey. (Though he was very low key about it, Dave had something close to organizational genius: he could have handled logistics for the moon shot.) Dave had a smart, sexy girlfriend who complained about him to us no end but adored him, and a magnificent collection of T-shirts, among which there was one with the words NO HEAD / NO BACKSTAGE PASS emblazoned across the front. Dave was in charge of backstage passes.

Did I agree with the commie polemics? Could I comprehend them? Well, yes to both, give or take. I'd had a course on the philosophical underpinnings of Marxism when I was at college. My teacher, a brilliant guy from Columbia who wore sunglasses inside and out, looked like a cross between Keith Richards and the large, expensively clipped poodle Pelops's parents owned. The poodle's name was Clarence, and he seemed to nurture bourgeois allegiances. When anyone set about leaving the apartment, he would bark imperiously and only stop when you informed him that you were on your way to Gristedes, a very pricey grocery store not far away, from which Clarence could reasonably expect gourmet dog treats.

Driving my cab, I chewed the Marxist thing over. The

world was a place rotten with injustice—on that I could concur. Even America—which was about all there was to *my* world at the time; I'd never left the country—stank with inequality. A few people had far too much; many had nothing. Marx proclaimed that such a state was an abomination; he declared that it must not last. This was so not only because capitalism ground the bones of the poor to make bread for the rich. Capitalism deformed everyone, even the privileged. Marx's sense of human promise, at least in the early work, has what seems a Renaissance origin. Human beings must not limit themselves to one sorry function; no one should become a "hand" in a factory, an "eye" minding the store, or a "brain" void of feeling. We shouldn't shrink ourselves to one role and become identical with a sole isolated and isolating task. Our destiny was larger than that. We should draw and paint and travel and write—and work, yes, but work at many different things, rather than at only one. We were, as Marx said in a moment of mild jocularity—never a common quality in Marx and rarer as time went by—to be hunters in the morning, fishermen in the afternoon, and "critical critics" at night. (On the matter of human fulfillment, Marx may have been trumped by his disciple, Trotsky. Asked what life would be like after the revolution, Trotsky replied that he wasn't sure, but he did suspect that people would need less sleep and sex would be much better.) Any economic arrangement that inhibits full human flourishing *must* change, or so the young Marx, the one who had only recently been a Romantic poet writing hymns to Prometheus the liberator of mankind, repeatedly claimed.

But there was a later Marx, I soon discovered, a long-bearded Old Testament prophet, raising his tablets overhead and preparing to throw them down on the free-marketers dancing around the golden calf, capitalism. The tablets this time weren't the Decalogue, commandments of the Lord, God of Israel, but *Das Kapital*, gift to the multitudes from the great god, Economic Science, and from its chief spokesman on earth, Karl Marx. I read all of the work, or almost all, or all I could, taking in installments when I pulled over at Willie's Bar and Grill on the Upper East Side. There I parked my cab and went in to restore myself with Willie's signature chili, so rich it seemed laced with bull's blood, and to empty a green flagon or two of Heineken. At Willie's I enlarged my consciousness about the dynamics of class conflict and of the *inevitability* of revolution from below. I sat so long at Willie's, studying the contradictions latent in the capitalist system, that I stopped earning much money with the cab. This put me in poor standing with the powers at Chad Taxi and Limousine Service, who hotly desired a piece of my earnings—far too large a piece, Marx told me.

The Marx of *Das Kapital* had repudiated his humanism: the word was no longer that things *ought* to change, given good intentions and humane energy and compassion, but that they *will*. The later Marx was enraged. He declared in the *Grundrisse*, the first draft, more or less, of the large-scale work on capital, that the bourgeoisie would pay for every one of the boils that he had developed on his backside while sitting in the British Library, laboring his way through old blue-booked industrial records, traveling deep inside the beast, capitalism, and filling his mind with facts, facts, facts. With those facts (or interpretations, as Nietzsche, in many ways his opposite number, would have been quick to tell him), Marx built himself a great catapult to launch his rock against things as they were. As surely as Babel had to crumble and Sodom and Gomorrah were destined to be dust, so the great cities of capitalism—including the one I now sat in ordering another beer I could barely afford, paying for it with nickels and dimes, my tip money—would soon go down. Revolution was on the way. Marx had a dialectic—his own magical three-phase system—and unlike Hegel's, it did not predict smooth synthesis, but class warfare, destruction, with regeneration to follow—whenever, whenever.

Was Marx turgid and humorless? Was he a hopeless puritan? Yes, yes, or so I saw it at the time. Was he also a hopeless conservative, who hated above all other things about capitalism its wild velocities of change? *The Communist Manifesto* is a testament to his fascination with, and fear of, capitalism as a mighty engine that speeds up time. It's as though he were watching a sedate, well-mannered film, but then minute by minute the rate of projection increases until the events begin to fly by in a whirlwind. Like Dorothy being whisked up by that tornado on the Kansas plains, Marx, sitting and pondering in the British Library, is pulled into a swirling force of wind himself. He's about to be spun to death by it, and not him alone. He sees nations and institutions and individuals rise and go to dust, at stunning velocity. Capitalism devours its young, and its old and middle-aged, too. So he protests: "Constant revolutionizing of production," he cries, "uninterrupted disturbance of all social conditions, ever-lasting uncertainty and agitation distinguish the bourgeois epoch from all previous ones. . . . All that is solid melts into air; all that is holy is profaned." What Marx wants is for time to slow down, for history to come to an end, for the "dictatorship of the proletariat" to arise and do away with the dizzying change.

So I encountered the iron-gray side of Marx, the part of

him that would have gone into apoplexy if he'd been dumped into the mud and grass at Woodstock when Country Joe & the Fish came onstage for the Fish cheer. ("Gimme an F! Gimme a U! Gimme a C! Gimme a K! What's that spell? What's that spell?") He would have been as angry with them in their decadence and debauchery as Abbie Hoffman was with the Who. Pelops, at least, wanted a good time. He wanted a revolution that you could twist and shout for. And Pelops was actually a ridiculously good dancer: people would stop in the middle of a party to watch him shake his whole three hundred, with rhythm nonpareil, and with exuberance and irony perfectly intermeshed.

With every arrogant character who stepped into my cab, Marx became more plausible, more my man. It wasn't only the guy who was cast into silence when he turned over my book and saw the old hoary lion head of Marx staring back at him. People were, and they probably still are, prone to treat the guy driving the cab as a servant. They bellowed orders; they addressed me as "driver"; they postured and declaimed. Most of the worst offenders, it seemed, were denizens of the Upper East Side, the bloated rich on whom Pelops planned one day to dine.

In democratic America, aristocracy is not dead. Even members of the middle class want to be temporary lords and ladies. They go out to restaurants and pretend that the greeter, the waitress, the cook, and the busboys are their personal servants. They boss them around the way a young nobleman out of Balzac would. They want to act big—as kids used to say in the schoolyard and probably still do. They do the same to elevator operators and drivers and functionaries of all sorts, who occasionally, to be sure, bite back. But did I say "they"? Even back during the cab-driving days, I was a temporary aristocrat myself from time to time, lolling at my ease at Willie's and occasionally summoning the bartender to pour another Heineken—though like most people who work for tips, I was regal with my gratuities: 30 percent, minimum.

But these are thoughts of the present. At the time, driving my cab, I had no pillowy speculations to account for what was going on when my passengers insulted me. No, what I mainly experienced was serial indignity. Often I fought back: If you called me "driver," I called you "passenger." If your manner was pompously heavy and your tip light, I might toss it back at you through my open window. ("I hope he treats you better than he treated me," a cabbie friend hollered out the window at a guy out with his date, after the guy stiffed him. I kept this comeback in my arsenal but never found the right moment.) If you tried to force your reactionary opinions on me, I would do five minutes on why Richard Nixon should be shaved, altered, caged, and put on exhibit next to the Washington Monument.

Yet sometimes, I have to admit, my class enemies gave as good as they got. One Sunday night, I picked up an old woman, brittle and spindly as a spider in early fall, when it's about to close accounts. She was standing under the awning of a mammoth building, a great gray elephant, on Park and Eighty-third or so. She gave her liveried doorman a tip (it looked to be a dime), then groaned her way into my backseat, closed the door, and said, in a voice I took to be somehow both snooty and vulgar, "Park and Fifty-second, driver, and step on it." Step on it! Were we in a 1950s movie? Did she think she was Lauren Bacall? Step on it! Driver!

I did. I banged the gas pedal in the stinking old Chevy so

hard that I found my two hundred or so pounds being thrown backward on the broken-springed seat. I felt like I'd been hit with a karate chop to the chest. As to what was happening to the matron in the backseat, I could only guess. I reveled in guessing.

We made maybe ten blocks, a good run, before the light changed. From the back, I heard the wiry, self-infatuated voice. "Driver, I must insist. I *am* in a hurry. Are you unable to go faster?"

When the light went green, I kicked my foot down as though I was trying to burst through the floor, and we launched. I went full tilt, weaving around the other cars, skimming and dodging like a bug on a lake. I was driving so fast I was terrifying myself. I ran two red lights, slinging my car around and through the others pushing east to west and west to east. They barked like outraged sea lions at me. When finally I saw the destination—it was a church—I cut for it so hard that I rolled the cab up and onto the curb, with a great thudding and burping of tires.

"Thank you, driver," my matron said. "We had a poor start, but then you made very good time." The fee was two dollars, and she gave me a 10 percent tip, twenty cents.

Maybe the rich are different. I recall one night, a Saturday, when fares were everywhere. They popped up all over the place, like targets in a shooting gallery, raising their imploring hands on what seemed like all corners. But some other cab always got there first; someone else stole my business. It was like a long frustration dream, with yellow goblins slashing in front of me and devouring the customers a moment before I reached them.

Things got so bad that I went to Times Square, which was

not the Disney emporium that it's become, but the infested heart of Sin City—peep shows, whores on the sidewalk, staggering sailors just in, fancy boys: sex, sex, sex. It was also filthy—all of New York was. The city, everyone knew, was on the brink of bankruptcy, petitioning for a federal bailout. President Ford listened to the entreaties and told the town to "Drop Dead!" Or so the *Daily News* translated his verdict. Everything seemed to have been left to the discretion of a purportedly omniscient money manager and general man-about-town called Felix "the Cat" Rohatyn. The understanding was that it was all up to Felix whether the city lived or died. Staring at Times Square through the window of my cab that night, it didn't look like the Cat's chances, or New York's, were too strong. Garbage was piled up in reeking Matterhorns in front of every restaurant; there was trash blowing up and down the streets; the place smelled like Chennai, India, in the early morning (not Chennai in the late afternoon; nothing smells like that). Times Square, never a center of learning and art, had all the charm of an infected, gently oozing wound.

A light turned yellow—no, now it was red, but I had to get across the street to snatch the fare on the far side. Cruising in the other direction—such that we seemed destined to meet at the center of the crucifix—was a plump Mercedes. It was swollen, limolike, and as it hove nearer, I saw that there was actually a chauffeur up front, capped and gloved. Behind him were what looked like mannequins in tuxes and gowns. I could almost hear their plastic arms click together; I could nearly make out their Tweety Bird voices. I looked back to the driver; his eyes were two tiny bonfires; he grinned a convict's grin. He came sliding at me, square and true. I jumped on the brakes with both feet, like a man leaping out a window, and my face went into what had to look like an electric-chair scream. He kept coming. He roared straight at me, fast and furious as a scheme flying through the devil's brain, and only stopped—his brakes were so well designed that they didn't make a sound—when his bumper kissed, ever so delicately, with Upper East Side refinement, the bumper of my yellow cab. The mannequins in the back stopped being mannequins, shed their plastic skin, and laughed like rock stars. The driver had shot the $20,000 prize in the direction of a junk heap that was worth not much more than the meager share of cash in my lockbox. He'd risked the beautiful bones of someone else's new Mercedes for a giggle.

This was an encounter with a phenomenon on which New York City probably corners the market. Call it rogue gentility, if you like. It's concentrated in the man who loves Mozart, Ferragamo ties, Burgundy of such and such a vintage, Chinese prints, and Aztec temple art, but can't breathe without exhaling the words *fuck*, *fucker*, *fucking*, *fuckee*, and the rest. Or there's the woman who drinks only the best champagne and insists on a top-tier designer for all her dresses, but squats to piss in the alley on the way home from her evening's revels. Or the guy who, exasperated at your lack of discernment, kicks you suddenly in the nuts with his handmade shoes. Maybe he'll goad his minion into almost scraping your cab with a new Mercedes so as to afford himself some diversion, then laugh like a rocker, laugh like a lion. Even Thoreau, who generally hated all things that smacked too much of civilization, said that there were some elevated natures who actually prospered in life's push and toss, getting more out of society than it managed to extract from them. Cultivated rogues, strong pagans, you might call them: high-style Romans in latter-day New York.

Vince Duggan's father was in his own way one of these types, and when I met him, I figured out where Duggan's bizarrely exuberant attitude toward driving a cab came from. Once, when Duggan's parents were heading off to Martha's Vineyard on vacation, Duggan invited me to come and stay with him at their apartment and indulge in an intense period of cab driving along with my rock-and-roll work. Cab driving made Duggan, who was usually in an insanely good mood, even happier. But Duggan's father was curious about his son's new pal. Who was this guy, anyway, to be staying in the Duggan manor on Park Avenue?

On the appointed day, I took the subway down the East Side to meet Senior and see if I couldn't get his OK. When I emerged into his neighborhood, I felt a cloud of mild depression descend. Poor Duggan! The buildings that lined Park Avenue looked homely and mournful to me. They were like the cathedrals of some tired old religious faith that had forgotten what it took to be beautiful and good. Someone had made off with the statues and the gargoyles and the stained glass and the flying buttresses and the rest, leaving these stripped-down shells. I thought back to my parents' cheery apartment outside of Boston, full of sunlight and potted flowers and the embroidered squares framed on the wall that welcomed guests and called down blessings on the house, and I felt a spark of pride.

The doorman at Duggan's place took a look at me in my rock uniform of jeans and boots and sent me around to the service elevator. I stepped in; he closed the metal crosshatch gate behind me and slid shut the door. The elevator began to ascend. It bumped and lurched like a big coffin being raised in the air. I felt that at any instant, the malicious doorman in his regimental suit might push a lever somewhere in the basement and send me down, down as though I and my coffin were being buried at sea. But it kept lurching and groaning upward. On the eleventh floor, the door opened, and I stepped out of my tomb into a grubby corridor, smelling of old linens and disinfectant. I pressed the bell. A rattling and banging of metal came from the inside, and Duggan appeared at the door, smiling his Duggan smile of incessant goodwill and Duggan optimism.

"Nice elevator," I said, gesturing back at the mobile coffin. This was the place where I was to have free room and board, and I was already insulting my host. Was I the type to look a gift horse in the mouth? No, no, I was prone to rear back and kick it good in the teeth.

"They're renovating the main one," Duggan told me. "Baryshnikov's moving into the building, and so they want it to look good."

"The fuck's Baryshnikov?" I asked. I sort of knew, but sort of didn't.

"Come on, you need to meet my father."

We walked into a small kitchen full of appliances that glowed like silver space modules. There were immaculate slabs of butcher block everywhere—it looked as though no one had ever chopped anything on them. Sitting at the kitchen table was Duggan Senior. He looked me up and down and smiled in a skeptical way. Clearly he was not much impressed. He held the smile for longer than was common or comfortable and I noticed the gleaming gold in his teeth; it echoed off the gold rings on his fingers and off the enormous cuff links he wore. Around his wrists, more gold: a bracelet, and a watch that must have weighed a pound. His nails were brightly buffed, too, and added to the illumination effect that came with the smile. It was as though he traveled with his own footlights and could flick them on as he chose.

"Where'd you get that beard?" Duggan Senior asked.

"Get it?"

"Yeah. It makes me think you should be in movies." Duggan Senior talked with great precision, enunciating every syllable, yet at the same time, he seemed to mock the precision. The effect was disconcerting.

"I don't mean on the screen," Senior continued. "I mean you should be in the dark, watching the movies, so no one has to see the beard." Duggan had a full growth as well, and I felt that Senior might be blaming me for his son's new rabbinical look. Senior's own cheeks had the vague bluish tinge of someone who shaves three times a day. "I got a new Norelco in my bathroom. Why don't you go down there and shave the thing off, OK?"

"I don't think so."

"Perhaps you'll change your mind," he said and gave me the shark smile. "Coffee?" Senior was drinking a cup so black that it might have taken the rust off an Edsel. Up on 187th Street, I'd been in training. No one could outblack me.

"Sure."

Senior drew back his lips and made a noise. "Nyeehhh" was what it sounded like. I took it to mean, *I approve*. Life is all bullshit, the sound said, but what we have here is bullshit less rank than most.

"So you and Vince are interested in cab driving?" he asked me.

I informed him that from what I could see, his son was interested in cab driving. I was interested in rent paying. Cab driving was a means to that end.

"Mistake," Senior declared. "That cab's a school. Teach you more than that fancy joint I'm paying a fortune for up in Vermont."

I told Senior that neither I nor my parents had paid Bennington much of anything.

Senior went on as if he hadn't heard me. He let me know that in that cab you could learn almost everything that mattered. It was a small business in itself; it gave you contact with people from all strata, taught you how to deal with them. If you could make a profit driving a cab and enjoy it, you could probably succeed in anything. "Whatever comes along," Senior declaimed, "get what you can. Learn what you can." You could tell that Senior, for all his dough, desperately wished that he could slide over to Queens and get a rig of his own.

I have to admit, I was curious. I asked questions. I showed interest. I had been living in the sixties for the last five years and more: I'd virtually never heard anyone get jazzed about the free market. Senior reciprocated. He revved up. He went into third gear reciting the Gospel according to Adam Smith and Horatio Alger. He talked to me about how intertwined were things like freedom of speech and freedom of movement and the free market. I bobbed my head.

"So you agree?" he asked me.

"I know I'm nodding," I told him. "But that just means I'm interested."

It was the right answer. If I'd told him I bought it all, he would have become bored: Senior needed some resistance to keep involved. I looked to him like a project—Senior loved nothing so much as a project. "Come on," he said after a pause. "Let's go downstairs and get some papaya, cut the grease." Then he said "Nyeehhh" again and started walking toward the back of the apartment, maybe for another shave.

In time I'd learn that Duggan Senior had been a poor boy himself. He'd scraped through Brooklyn College, working a string of jobs on the side, and then he'd gone to law school at night. Though he dearly loved being an imperial New Yorker, he was probably happier when he was young and on the make. He thrived on having his back close to the wall, savored trying to make something of nothing. In this, Duggan Senior took after his own father, who was not short on resources. During the Depression, Senior's father had lost his job. What to do? He had some musical talent and played the piano, so he decided to go into business giving music lessons. He put an ad in the paper, proclaiming that he could teach any instrument. When a kid's parents called to say that they'd like their son to start up on, say, the flute, Senior's father stopped by their house and informed them he wanted a look at the instrument. The flute was OK, he told them, but it badly needed cleaning. So Senior's father took it home over the weekend and began learning to play it. He worked on it fourteen hours at a stretch. By Monday, he was ready to give a lesson.

"How about that Norelco?" Senior called from over his shoulder.

"Maybe later."

"Alright."

Duggan and I followed his father out of the kitchen into a long dark hallway and stood to wait for him. I glanced to the right and saw a living room bigger than my parents' entire apartment. There were four chairs at one end of the room, majestic in design, as though ready to receive four latter-day sages there to ponder humanity's collective future. There was a bookcase that held at least a thousand volumes, many richly bound and embossed, as though for the library of a Venetian doge. On the wall were African masks, fierce in design and expression, creating, in their apparent savagery, a rich contrast to the civilizing books and the calmly patterned Oriental rugs on the floor.

Duggan Senior reappeared, and soon the three of us had piled into the rumbling coffin and were headed down amid a rasping and sighing of machinery.

"Front elevator's being renovated," Senior explained.

"They'd have put me on this one anyway," I said.

"The super's a prick," Senior replied. His voice was softer now, instructional. "You'll have to watch out for him. The rest of the crew is OK, though. Ask them about baseball. They're all Dominicans."

That night of the Mercedes kiss, I got into a real accident.

I still needed fares: it was ten o'clock or so, and I'd booked about twelve dollars. I saw a couple of prospects: two elderly guys, black, clearly drunk, wobbling and doddering at a curbside in Times Square.

When I'd first arrived at Chad Taxi and Limousine Services, a couple of old hands took me aside and gave me what they took to be the one crucial piece of advice for a new driver. "Don't pick up blacks. Don't do it. They'll rob you, or they'll beat you for the fare, and if they do pay, they'll never tip." This advice went for everyone who was African American— businessmen, actors, athletes, sharp dressers or drab: simply don't stop and let them in your cab, period. The experienced younger drivers were more nuanced in their take, a little. "Don't pick up blacks in sneakers," they said. "Other than that, it's basically OK." So there was a no-sneaker rule. At least neither the young guys nor the old called black people *niggers*, a word constantly in the air in the Irish-Italian neighborhood I'd grown up in north of Boston.

To my credit, small but real enough, I did not follow either of these rules. Miles Davis, asked why he let white people play in his band, replied, "I don't care if the dude is purple with green breath, as long as he can swing." (But he did have the temerity to call the splendid Bill Evans a good little white piano player.) Well, I didn't care if you were orange or white or brown or black or yellow or blue; if you hailed my cab, I picked you up. I picked up black kids in sneakers all the time. Once I took six of them, twelve-year-olds, to the South Bronx—home of the Savage Skulls and other purportedly vicious street gangs—and when we got close to a vacant lot and I stopped, they all ran like wild mice. Before they skipped, though, one of them tried to explain to me how to get back to Manhattan.

Mostly, the black kids in sneakers paid. On two separate occasions, though, white businessmen, decked out in suits and apparently chained to their briefcases and respectability, bolted out of my cab at traffic lights, leaving me to pay for them. But just about everyone I picked up paid, though the number, male and female, who offered me fellatio in lieu of the fare, usually less than five bucks, would give most any moralist pause. The only customers I was inclined to think twice about picking up were drunks, whatever color they might be. I mean reeling, stumbling, blubbering, gurgling drunks—drunks about to pass out. Whatever problems they had, and inevitably they had plenty, quickly became mine.

The guys hailing me on this night were truly reeling, stumbling, blubbering, and gurgling. But it was getting late,

I'd made no money to speak of, and though there were fares everywhere, I couldn't manage to get them. It was a little like the way Kafka describes it: "Oh, plenty of hope, an infinite amount of hope—but not for us." There were fares, no end of fares—but not for me.

Though on this night I was desperate, there were times when I savored nothing so much as being alone in my cab. I loved cruising around Manhattan, genially ignoring a fare or two, moving very deliberately, taking it all in like a hyper-mobile flaneur out to explore the city. Alone in the cab, I could look and wonder, look and wonder. Yet better than cruising softly on my own was finding myself still on the street at four o'clock in the morning when the traffic was in its hour-or-two phase of remission. I'd make my way over to Sixth Avenue. (Duggan nearly imploded when I called it the Avenue of the Americas. "What do you call Seventh Avenue? Fashion Ave?") I'd cruise as far downtown as I could, then turn north and sit patiently waiting for the first light to go green, then the light ahead of it and the next and the next. I'd pop the gas and begin moving north, driving almost as fast as the Chevy would go, but not fast enough to outrace the lights as they flicked green one after another. It was like being a surfer, riding the edge of a wave, cruising fast, never easing on the pedal, never stopping until I came to Central Park. At which point, I often drove back downtown and did it again. If you happened to hail my cab during a Sixth Ave Surf, I'm sorry, there was no way I was going to stop for you.

But this night in Times Square, all the joys of solitary cab driving were in abeyance. When at last the black guys appeared, waving, laughing, and falling over each other as cabs streamed by them on all sides, I had to go for them. No one wanted to pick them up, so there was no reason why I bolted another intersection. But I was desperate for a fare and humiliated by the Mercedes driver and his clutch of malice-bearing mannequins, so again I pushed the gas, when I should have waited and cruised gently in.

How my cab got tagged from behind, I can't say. I never felt much impact. Somehow, someone's bumper ticked the edge of my own at exactly the right angle, and I was spinning like a clock, a compass—or better, a roulette wheel—in the middle of Times Square. All the dirty neon, all the color, the whores and pimps and sailors, the pavement and the windows and the signs created quite a blur. What number was I going to stop on? Would it be the one that brought contact full force with another vehicle and left me maimed and my cab a carcass? The one that took out a harmless pedestrian?—if anyone in Times Square that night could be called harmless. Luckily the wheel stopped on zero. Nothing. I made no contact at all. After at least two revolutions, I was again pointing in the direction of my two fares-to-be, who were laughing so hard, in such throes of theatrical appreciation for the great scene that they had witnessed and partly created simply by the raising of a hand, that each was vying with the other for who would get to collapse and who would have to provide support. "Man, you did desire this fare," one of them hollered as he tumbled into the backseat, loose as a half sack of flour.

I took them where they wanted to go, and at the end, they gave me what I'd come to think of as the cabdriver's Pulitzer, a 100 percent tip. After that, the rest of the evening went pretty well. The two guys were blues musicians, or said they were, off for the night, and they were funny and easygoing. Whatever they were all about, neither one seemed to have a drop of malice in him. Whereas malice, if my night's experience—maybe my overall experience in the cab—was representative, was what the rich were often all about. Eat them at your peril, Pelops: to the digestive track they'd be no balm.

The truth is that from then to now I've hardly met a rich person who seemed to have much gift for happiness. I saw the rich up close at Bennington College, when I was a student, and I taught their children at Yale, where I was becoming a doctor of philosophy and acquiring subtle ideas. While I drove a cab, I saw them from a bit further below, which is almost never a flattering angle. No man is a hero to his valet, to be sure, but his driver may see an even more unpleasant side. The driver, after all, is a means to an end—he gets the more privileged personage from one place to another. So it's almost impossible not to see the driver as a piece of machinery, and not fully human. Kant said that the great moral mistake was being unwilling to regard other people as ends in themselves, but to see them instead as ways of achieving one's goals. At that point, when a person becomes a mere conductor, he disappears. But that's an advantage in a way: you see and hear many things when you become invisible; you're like a low-rung spirit sojourning unseen on the earth.

What I've encountered in almost every prosperous person I've met, both in the confines of my cab and outside, is an anxiety that almost passes understanding. How shall I live up to my wealth? Am I buying the right things? Am I preserving them adequately? Do others think me a moneyed nonentity? What the hell did I do with the keys to the summer house?

The rich often lead a twitching Saint Vitus' dance of a life because they have material anxieties in spades—they've got more affairs, more domiciles and cars, more stuff to worry about. People in the process of making their fortunes are often having a fine time of it. They know where to aim their energies, and lo, their efforts are rewarded in the only absolute currency we know, which is currency itself.

The psychoanalyst Adam Phillips speculates that the desire for money—money pure and simple, not what it will buy— might be a way not to think about our other desires. Why shouldn't we want to ponder all of our desires? Because many of them are disturbing. They have their origins in childhood, Phillips tells us. And in childhood we simply want what we want. We may want love and more love, or love of a disturbing sort—dominating love or submissive, gay love or group love or what have you. The engines of control inside and out don't approve of these things. They don't want us to want them. So along comes the hunger for money to stand between us and more wayward wants—to stand between us and knowing ourselves.

Yet while a person is stockpiling money and too distracted to spend it, he can be as happy as a human can be, at least from what I've seen. Happiness, it's been said, is absorption in something you love, and the makers of money are often deeply absorbed. Perhaps, too, money can be a fine way to keep score in life, though only if you're winning.

This at least seemed to be the way that Duggan Senior took things: he was always on the go, always on the make. He would have deeply approved of Emerson's observation that "power ceases in the instance of repose." True power, Emerson thought, "resides in the moment of transition from a past to a new state, in the shooting of the gulf, in the darting to an aim." Senior was almost always in motion himself. And he added to his vigor by allying himself with other people's attempts at enlivening change. He liked to coach them as they darted to their aims and shot their gulfs and all the rest.

Senior was an inveterate giver of presents, and during the first year he knew me, he constantly gave me cab-related stuff. He got me a coin changer; he gave me a box of receipt books and offered me instructions on how to tailor the receipts to the customer's needs; he got me a mechanical pencil because the one I recorded my trips with was forever breaking. To Duggan he gave even more such things. But what Senior couldn't convey to me was his absolute love for the roiling ocean, full of creatures thriving and dwindling, that was capitalism. Senior was blissfully at home there: he swam through it like a fishy emperor and wanted me and Duggan to learn to do the same. But I didn't have the stuff for it. Had I made money, I fear I would have been what Senior so grandly was not: a sterile rich man, a Silas Marner gloating over his pile. When I read an essay in which T. S. Eliot commended the poet's "necessary laziness," I knew that, whether I could ever turn a metaphor or not, I had at least one ingredient for the gig. I was—and still often can be—a world-class doer of nothing at all for grandly extended periods. Rich, I'd probably think myself a king and go comatose. I'd be like a guy sitting on the highest pile in the town dump, sceptered with an old rolled-up newspaper and crowned with a bucket. Money? To me, it was Death in Life. Money, despite Senior's eloquence, probably wasn't *it* for me.

Still, I've no doubt that it's important to have the rich around, for they illustrate consequential points. They show us what is and is not possible for someone who can have everything he wants. They do some remarkable things, the rich.

They buy boats and watches, islands and penthouses—and then are made, if not sadder, at least tighter and more watchful. Those two guys falling all over each other in Times Square lived in the present, a place the rich almost never get to visit, absorbed as they are in acquiring and maintaining and worrying about it all. If one is born beautiful, one has no reason to strive—the world will pay you attention anyway; so once wealthy, there is little reason to struggle, either. Boredom is not as deadly as extreme want, but in the long run it can do some of the same nefarious things.

I loved Pelops no end and esteemed him, too. But sometimes I half thought that the King of Rock and Roll resented his parents, who expected so much from him, almost as much as he loved the thought of revolution. Have you ever met a middle-class revolutionary who did not seem to have difficulties with his bourgeois mom and dad? I have, but not too often. Generally, when they're talking about the workers and the peasants and the power structure and all its wrongs, you hear the humorless intensities of the old family feuds. Frequently, I have to say, I agree with much of the message— no more bread from the bones of the poor!—but the manner sends me reeling away, my teeth on edge. There's no doubt in my mind: the dispensation of wealth and opportunity in the world, even in the nation, are often a horror. But those who would deliver us from it often do not bode so well either.

Somehow or other, I got Duggan interested in Marxist polemics. He acquired all the books and read a few, too. He became adept in discussing "alienation," "contradiction," and "class struggle." Senior heard it all and took it in. He pondered it in his rare paternal way. But he launched no counter-oration at Duggan about the joys of the free market. He didn't buy the collected works of Milton Friedman and drop them on the threshold of his son's room. Instead he bought Duggan a little blue Mao cap with a stylish red star pinned at the center, glowing like the Buddhist third eye, the eye of enlightenment. Duggan wore it around for a while, calling out "Hi, Tiny" and "Tiny, how's it going?" from beneath the soft blue dome. A wise father, Duggan Senior: his son is now a large-scale success, genial and generous.

Pelops wanted a new father for himself, I sometimes think: he wanted whiskery old Karl Marx to descend from on high and turn the brutal, color-drenched, glamorous world of the market, the chaos bazaar, into a slower, fairer, grayer operation, where no one bothered him about going to law school. Pelops wanted justice—I have no doubt about that; there was something pure in his soul (somewhere)—but I think he also wanted to inform the world how angry he was for what it demanded from him. As to my laughing, generous drunks: they would have had it no better in the workers' paradise than they did in fallen, greedy America, and probably they would have had it worse. The commissars could never have forgiven them their Saturday nights.

And me? The life of the rich man wasn't my game, but what about the thing Thoreau called "voluntary poverty"? It's possible that, not for the last time, my ineptitude saved me. I could never have driven skillfully enough to make ends meet and taken up a life of dignified asceticism—driving a cab and becoming, in what spare time there was, a fierce autodidact, haunting the cafeterias and buttonholing younger guys, in the style of the Ancient Mariner, to tell them about the Revolution. I was too dreamy and curious not to try something new and was probably, on some level, too ambitious to subordinate myself to any collective program. When Duggan's father bought me a Mao hat, with the red eye of enlightenment on the forehead, I thanked him, admired the gift, but never quite found the moment to put it on.

A MOVIEGOER

(jobs)

At a certain point, Duggan and Duggan Senior began to believe that there was something wrong with me. They thought that I was exhibiting a dismal attitude. I wasn't going at life with Duggan-style vigor, bringing joyous warlike passion to my day-to-day business. They felt that something needed to be done.

Maybe they were right. I had some fine times working at the rock shows, and I could even savor a shift or two in the cab, though not much more than that. But things often grew dismal on 187th Street and stayed that way for days running. Pelops would lock himself up with the classics; Dave spent six hours and more on the phone, meeting the demands and buffing the egos of the members of this rock band and that. I sat upstairs trying to write. (Pelops began calling me Homer in honor of my efforts.) But I had no idea what I was supposed to be writing. In college, I'd taken a liking to Joyce's *Ulysses*, which I only half understood. I assumed that most of the book was stream of consciousness, pure free association. So I let the mental waters flow, slamming away on my electric typewriter, creating the impression of an inspired verbal stampede. But in the end, all I had was stuff that even I could recognize was rubbish. Eventually my typewriter, tired of having to rave all day, shut down and would type no more. When I turned it on, it squatted there in front of me, humming autistically.

Looking out my dirt-smeared window onto dirty 187th Street, I had plenty of reason to be melancholy, at least as I saw it. It was early on in the game, but already I'd made significant errors. I had made the mistake of *graduating* from Bennington College, the school that had funded me with that massive scholarship. The place kept me housed and fed. I never quite got over my joy at the all-you-could-eat aspect of college dining. Emaciated dancers would approach my table, their plates holding small abstract-art installations composed of green beans and carrot shavings, and stare at my plate mounded with rice and pasta and beef and say, breath quivering, "You're going to *eat* that?" (Oh yeah—and go back for seconds, too.) Bennington was full of gorgeous, smart, tightly wound women, in the proportion of three to every one male; the teachers were surpassingly hip; the Vermont green was seven versions of pastoral. In the middle of springtime nights, I woke up to hear post-Coltrane jazz honking and sliding through air, which was thick with the smell of lilacs. (One afternoon, I heard the music's main instigator, a jazzman with about fifty winters on his head, talking in his raspy nightclub voice behind one of the dorm-room doors. He was repeating, as if they composed a magic spell, the words, "You are, you know, one of the most sensitive white persons I have ever encountered." There were responsive purrs, then, after six or so repetitions of the spell, happy moaning and panting.)

The students at Bennington were rich and a little loopy: they were, it seemed, frequently the youngest children of prosperous, prominent parents. But apparently the kids had often been ignored by Mom and Dad, who perhaps were absorbed in making their way through Alex Comfort's *Joy of Sex* (second cousin to the *Joy of Cooking*), with each other and with neighbors and friends, praying that they hadn't missed all the rapture the sixties had to dispense. The Bennington parking lot was bumper-to-bumper with BMW 2002s and Saabs that looked like benign extraterrestrials. Why would anyone want to leave such a place?

My roommate, Victor, who understood that he had landed in paradise, spent about six years at the college. He tried a half dozen majors: musical instrument design was one of them, as was, he claimed, advanced bicycle repair. He formed close if temporary bonds with many women, including a princess and a president's great-grandniece—one of the solemn, whiskery Ohio presidents, alas. When it became clear to Victor that I was voluntarily leaving this Eden after only four years of college, total, he wrote me off as mentally ill.

Now, scraping down the pavement in New York on one of my days off from rock and driving the cab, I had to admit that Victor probably had it right. New York sent many signs to a young man like me—it was an empire of signs, to cop a phrase—but one message blared through and over all the rest: This city (state, country, world, cosmos) does not require you at all. No provisions have been made. There is no slot. I recalled a poem by Stephen Crane that I'd come across in junior high: "A man said to the universe, / 'Sir, I exist.' / 'However,' replied the universe, / 'The fact has not created in me / A sense of obligation.'" I occasionally thought of another line, too, one that I'd fetched up from the crammed commonplace books that Victor filled with quotations, drawings, and photographs: "If nothing comes, then nothing comes. This isn't exactly the enchanted forest." Which was true enough: New York City, in the mid-1970s, especially up in Washington Heights, was not the enchanted forest.

One gets used to having a slot, however meager. For sixteen years there had been a seat reserved for one M. Edmundson at some center of higher or lower learning. Mark E., who sat behind Kevin Donahue and in front of Joan Ehlrich, in homeroom at Medford High School was present or he was absent. Absence mattered. Inquiries would be made. Now there was neither presence nor absence. There was zip. No one was taking attendance. If I'd failed to show up at the cab garage, nobody would have noticed. If I'd stopped answering crew calls in Jersey, Dave would have noticed but ultimately wouldn't have cared. (Stage-crew work was something a lot of people wanted and which, overall, I wasn't terribly good at.) I had nursed hopes, as the poet says, that pointed to the stars. There was Bennington and the great concert at Woodstock; and there were the Beatles and the Stones and that post-Coltrane jazz. Now I was a walking superfluity, a flea on New York's shaggy, rank-smelling coat.

Uptown and downtown, New York was absurdly dirty and chaotic: There was graffiti everywhere, but especially on the subway cars. The squeegee guys were massed at significant corners, ready to descend on cars like locust swarms when the light turned red. They often hit my cab, for want of a more lucrative target, and left the windshield greasier than it had been before, which was not an easy trick. There were broken windows everywhere. The cops hadn't yet become helpful public servants, joshing and dispensing directions; they were truculent and profane and sometimes pretty funny. The younger ones stood on the corners, never walking, twirling their batons and hitting on the girls who strolled past. Once when I was on the subway heading to the garage in Queens, I saw two subway cops who'd grown particularly ashen and grim underground, like a couple of Morlocks out of H. G. Wells. They were observing a gaggle of Kansas-aura tourists wearing shorts and sun hats; two were wagging American flags. One of the cops looked in my direction: "Hey, why don'tcha do something constructive?" he said. "Go mug those characters."

Going out for groceries, I had to cross the street an extra couple of times so as not to pass the local drug corners, which started humming at about three in the afternoon and stayed open, with no interference I could discern, until four in the morning. I'd see them knocking off and calling it a night when I rose up like a blackened specter from the subway after a long shift in my cab. How was it possible that, staying inside a vehicle, I could get as filthy as I inevitably did?

We were at perpetual war with our landlord, whom Pelops and Dave held to be a crook. When Pelops looked out onto the street and saw the guy—whom he called, in what I took to be high Marxist fashion, "the landlord element" or at times simply "the element"—he pushed open the window and hollered invective at him, sometimes about conditions in the apartment (the shower never worked; the stove rarely) and sometimes about matters that were vaguely extraterrestrial. One time, I saw Pelops slam down the window in midsentence—*ker-pow*—

and when I asked him why, he told me that five minutes of running denunciation was all a landlord deserved and that he'd hit the limit.

New York was dirty and chaotic, but it was in its strange way a paradise, and this, too, I sometimes recognized. The wild division between rich and poor hadn't fully set in, so there was a feeling that almost everyone was in the same boat. Real estate was reasonably cheap—with the sole exception, it sometimes seemed, of our apartment, which was pricey as well as ugly, inconvenient, and dangerously placed—and so people could show up in New York and begin painting or writing without having to spend all their time making ends meet, eventually getting swallowed up in some job they didn't want. The fact that the damned subway trains were always stopping between stations, with the lights sometimes cutting out; that you saw rats dancing like popping corn on the track up ahead of you; and that the cars themselves made the noise of ungreased apocalypse as they came into the station were all reasons for exchanging a look of soldierly commiseration with the guy or gal beside you in the fetid gray box. Sometimes a conversation actually began. Most people seemed to think that the graffiti was a plague, but if you liked it, as I sometimes did, there was often a mobile art gallery coming your way. "You're standing there in the station, everything is grey and gloomy," the artist Claes Oldenberg said, "and all of a sudden one of those graffiti trains slides in and brightens the place like a big bouquet from Latin America." Sometimes, anyway.

Still, there were plenty of bad days. A lot of my Bennington classmates, who had downplayed their cash and connections at college, were redeeming these previously invisible chips.

Pelops had been right about them when he'd informed me that they weren't leaving college to hang out. They had plans in place. They latched on to cool internships; they hit cocktail parties uptown and down where they augmented their stock of connections. My former teachers—broke on their laughable Bennington salaries, in hock because of their midlife late-sixties divorces—paid court to *them*, their onetime students, cadging weekend couches in their living rooms and invitations to openings at galleries like OK Harris. As for me, being broke and precariously employed and vaguely promising didn't fork a lot of lightning.

Duggan and his father had a solution for my woes, and it wasn't the cultivation of proletarian class consciousness that Pelops endorsed. What I needed, according to them, was a job. They meant a real job, something that I showed up for five days a week, that drew on my college-cultivated talents (whatever those might be), and that involved a desk, a salary, and room for advancement. Duggan and Senior would sit me down and wax rhapsodic about the virtues of jobs and fill my tank with Duggan-style hope. Why shouldn't they be all in favor of such things? If Senior, or even Duggan himself, who was all of nineteen, had started on Monday as a Fuller Brush man, schlepping cartons of samples door-to-door, after the passage of around thirty Mondays, they'd own a chunk of the company; in a few years, the place would be theirs outright. As for me, I was nearly certain that no straight job would ever yield the great good thing that on some level I still secretly yearned for. Yet Duggan and his father managed to be so in love with life as it was that I'd catch hold of their hopes for me for a while and imagine that they might become mine.

My parents were also worried. Just as she had when I was

in college, my mother sent me a box of food every two weeks, to ensure that I wouldn't dip below my two-hundred-pound prime, and with these boxes there came notes. My mother was honestly perplexed that her son, who had gone to the highest-priced college in America (which neither she nor anyone in my neighborhood had ever heard of until I applied), was driving a cab and slinging amps for a living. I told her that I was trying to become a writer, and there were those days, now past, when I'd made my electric typewriter rip like a firing squad. But she asked me to send her some of what I had written. Though she'd only been to high school, my mother was a great reader and had a serene confidence in her literary judgments. She once read a few novels by Henry James on my recommendation and pronounced him "not such a much." It didn't seem a good idea to send her my stream-of-consciousness innovations.

My father was a great example to me in many ways, though I sometimes think the major lesson he taught was: Do what you please. Consult no other being. This is not the worst counsel to have at certain moments, but as a Golden Rule, it has its drawbacks. My father was not a hands-on dad. Once, when I was about ten, we were driving by a heavily fortified brick building a few blocks from our home in Malden, Massachusetts. He exhaled Camel cigarette smoke through his grand nose, a nose to equal Charles De Gaulle's, he sometimes bragged, and inquired what the building might be. I told him that it was my elementary school, Belmont. He tried to compensate for this gap in his knowledge with a show of enhanced paternal interest. This took the form of asking me what grade I happened to be in at the time. My father dearly loved me and my brother, of that I have no doubt; he was simply not prone to details. But my mother was, and she was disturbed by what I was making of my expensive education, which, to be sure, we had acquired at a deep discount. (For Bennington, I had paid the Filene's Basement price.) She was worried, too, about my happiness. When I told her I was beginning to be interviewed for jobs in the publishing world, she expressed great relief.

Pelops disapproved of the entire job idea. He told me that what my kind friends saw as mild depression was actually a healthy dose of alienation. Anybody who wasn't at least a touch miserable under the current conditions wasn't paying attention: humanity was suffering and one was compelled to be mournful about it, at least some of the time. Only a bourgeois individualist, who cared exclusively about himself, could go larking through life in its current state. Pelops admitted that he liked Duggan (everybody liked Duggan) but said that Duggan was still a member of the overclass.

"Will you devour him when the time comes to eat the rich?" I asked.

"There will be tribunals. He will face revolutionary justice like all the rest," Pelops said, half smiling. I looked at him with great sadness, for Duggan was very dear to me. Pelops relented a little. "Who knows? Maybe we'll eat him last."

Duggan and his father went ahead making plans for getting me a job, and I more or less acquiesced. Maybe I could go into journalism, Duggan's game. With Duggan, I collaborated on pieces for the *Village Voice Centerfold*. The *Centerfold* was a double page at the middle of the paper that ran reviews of offbeat restaurants, announcements for shows at offbeat galleries, previews of offbeat movies, et cetera. There was also usually a feature piece in the middle, taking up this or that angle on life in New York. Duggan and I composed these from time to time, and one of them, conceived by Duggan, who harbored a surprising willingness to cause trouble, created a small ruckus. It was on the best places to take a piss in New York if you had no money and couldn't duck handily into a restaurant and order something cheap. The absolute best place turned out to be the men's room in the Plaza Hotel, where for whatever reason the staff didn't hassle you. But on the way to our ultimate verdict, we surveyed other sites, including the men's room at the Port Authority Bus Terminal, which we judged a highly convenient if slightly dangerous option. We recommended it but counseled speed. Our sign-off line for the Port Authority section was "Zip, Whizz, Zip: Adios." The editor of the piece, Helena Michaud, nearly got fired for running it. Clay Felker, who owned the *Voice* at the time, also owned *New York* magazine. He thought that our article was written to parody the consumerist idiocy—where do you buy the best dog sweater in the city?—that made *New York* (and I suppose much of New York, too) rattle and go. Perhaps in some way our piece was exactly that, though if you've ever been broke in New York and looking a little ratty, you'll know it was more than that, too. I adored Helena, who treated me and Duggan like worldly wise writers when we were nothing of the kind, and I was sorry we endangered her job, but of course I was also pleased to have pissed off the authorities. I couldn't tell Pelops about it: he would have described our salvo as "merely epiphenomenal," carbonated fizz where real explosions were needed.

Did Pelops himself provide real explosions? About his political exploits, he was remarkably silent. But a tale did trickle up to the apartment about a demonstration at Columbia where he had snatched a lead role. The demonstration was against the university's investments in apartheid-ridden South Africa. "Cut your ties!" the protestors chanted. "Cut your ties!" The idea was to get Columbia to stop all investments in companies that did business with the Johannesburg government. Pelops, it seemed, did the standard demonstrators one better. "Cut your ties," he and his coterie supposedly shouted at the trustees and administrators, "or we'll cut them for you!" "Cut your ties," they said, "or *we'll* cut your ties." And after the meeting, where no tie-cutting resolutions passed, they did exactly that. The Pelops clique approached the suited miscreants and, with small pairs of scissors, cut their ties at the midpoint—quick acts of castration. When I asked Pelops about the caper, he did his leonine frown, shuffled, and laughed but—a near first for Pelops—would say not a word.

Helena Michaud was greatly admired and pursued by what seemed like the majority of the male editors in the New York publishing world. I walked into her office one day for nothing in particular—you were always welcome to walk into Helena's office for nothing in particular—and she showed me a note from a former boyfriend. "Let's tryst again like we did last summer," it read. "Let's tryst again, like we did last year." I asked if there would be some summer trysting. Helena predicted that there would be, but not with this particular doggerelist, who over the winter had revealed himself to be a married man.

Duggan managed to enlist Helena in the quest to get me installed in a real job, and he could not have found a better co-conspirator. When she called to tell this or that male editor that there was a young man he just had to meet, the call recipient would swallow hard, say OK, then ask Helena out for a drink. She went off on some of these dates, too, not only for her own purposes but out of kindness for me. In between coming up with ideas for the *Centerfold*, she and Duggan schemed to get me a life.

I wasn't uninterested: I listened to their plans for me, got a little jazzed about the new interview, and felt no end of gratitude to them both. But mostly what I wanted to do during those open gray afternoons in New York was to go to the movies. Even if there was no real place for me in Manhattan— no chair with my name on it—at least there was always a seat, unoccupied if not specifically assigned, stained with Coke, crackling with popcorn bits, at the movies. When I told Senior that I was hitting a lot of movies, he informed me that he was happy to go with his wife, who enjoyed them, but that he generally went to sleep a minute or two in. Senior had a knack for going to sleep at opportune times, times when there was no action. Given a reasonable inducement, he was capable of staying awake for a week.

At first, I went for predictable fare. I liked to see Clint Eastwood clean out nests of grungy crooks—crooks only marginally grungier than he was. I liked Jack Nicholson, who was busy turning himself from a Jersey guy into a Carl Jung archetype of hipness. De Niro, Pacino, and Nicholson were my blessed trinity for a while: they were elegantly alienated— not angrily, sadly alienated the way Pelops wanted me to be. I caught their movies, and my heart swelled. I was them and they were me: all was superbly right in the world, at least for the couple of hours that I was sitting there watching. But then I discovered Robert Altman, and my sense of what movies (and maybe life) might be all about changed.

When one of the deep-downtown movie emporia announced an Altman festival, I was up by noon on the inaugural day. I pulled on my Frye boots, my jeans with the blue unworn rectangle on the thigh (where my backstage pass for the rock shows always went), and my red Capitol Theater T-shirt with the white star on the back, *Stage Crew*. I said good-bye to my electric typewriter and all its afflictions and to my poster of Patty Hearst, posing with a machine gun and her fellow members of the Symbionese Liberation Army. "The people," ran the legend below the photo: "We have been nothing, we shall be all." Pelops had given the poster to me as a gift, so I felt that I had to put it up. (When a guy from the phone company came to the apartment to install a telephone, he looked at Patty and Cinque and the gang, then turned and walked down the stairs and into the street. No phone for us.) Soon I was on the subway, with my book, Deutscher's biography of Trotsky, flying downtown to Altman.

Altman was a debunker, but of a certain sly sort. He liked to take the air out of standard genres: detective movies, buddy flicks, cowboy and Indian things, even, in a way, musicals (I'm thinking of *Nashville*). He ran against the great tendency of film, which is to glamorize everything. Film makes Olympians out of mere mortals, surrounding each star with a glowing aura. And of course it expands them until they're deific in size, or at least parental. In general, we go to the movies to see giant forms; we go to traffic with gods.

What I loved about Altman was how he cut against this glamour with his crisscross layer-on-layer dialogue, his low-to-the-ground camera, and his muzzy action sequences. What the hell is happening in about half of *McCabe and Mrs. Miller*? I couldn't figure it out, even though I sat through the thing five times. Yet still I believed I'd never seen a better movie.

What Altman discovers is that life seen from the edges is not glamorous, not alluring, but constantly fascinating. People are small, they want petty things, but because of that they're very tender and easily hurt. In *The Long Goodbye*, the hard-boiled detective's ridiculous affection for his cat—his determination, against all odds, to get him precisely the right cat food—truly moved me.

I felt the same way about the scene in *McCabe and Mrs. Miller* when Warren Beatty, as an Old West entrepreneur who's slick and bumptious at the same time, runs a monologue about how he, despite all appearances, has poetry in him: "Ain't gonna try to put it down on paper . . . got sense enough not to try." (Maybe I felt I had some poetry in me, too, but I knew that if I'd tried to get it down on paper, Pelops would have firebombed my room. Two subjects that could launch him into orbit were contemporary lyric poetry and impressionist painting.) Altman's camera—ignored, roaming, left to itself—achieves a sort of freedom. The camera doesn't need to aggrandize life, but it doesn't need to offer resentful rejections, either. It seems to accept all it encounters, taking it in with an affectionate eye, gently curious about what will come next but not exerting itself unduly to find out. Altman's camera, Altman's eye, manages to be both in and out of the game, watching and wondering at it.

And might not this be a little like my own condition, or at least one that I could aspire to during those grimy days in New York? I could amble and loaf and look around and maybe store up a few impressions. I was *near*-broke most of the time, sure, but I had enough to get by. My pockets were almost always jangling with change from the cab. What I had in plenty was what Altman and his camera seem to have—time and a fascinating place to spend it, Manhattan, the greatest paradise for walkers and loiterers and ramblers yet created. Looking—affectionately, gently, looking around—turned out to be a not half-bad way of expanding the day.

So during the hours when I was supposed to be out searching for a job or getting my résumé typed or working the pay phone to make connections, I rambled around. I checked out the neighborhoods. I kibitzed with people hanging out on their stoops, though I'm not a readily sociable type. I walked across the Brooklyn Bridge strung, as Hart Crane says, like a great lyre over the water: "O harp and altar, of the fury fused," he chants, "(How could mere toil align thy choiring strings!)." When I reached the other side, I got myself lost in Brooklyn. For a while, getting lost became my game. When I didn't know where I was or where I was going, the colors of things seemed to heighten; the music coming from the radio perched in the tenement window—even though it wasn't *my* music—became a dissonant sound track to my walk, stimulating moods I didn't know I could have. I covered Central Park up and down; I went and loitered where I wasn't supposed to go, to black Harlem and to Spanish Harlem, too. Craving Chinese food one afternoon, I walked from the Upper East Side down to Chinatown, about six miles. (I brought back a container for Pelops, who loved the stuff. By the time I got home, it was oozing yellow juice.) I even began liking—or trying to like—a few things about our neighborhood, Washington Heights. The only thing I shied away from were official sites for looking, like museums and galleries, Radio City Music Hall and the Statue of Liberty: all else was fair game.

I made it a never-articulated point to like everything, or as much as possible of everything, that I saw—though not to like it too very much, because when you fall for one thing, be it a beautiful bridge, a beautiful building, or a beautiful body or soul, everything else gets demoted and has to take a backseat.

In my head, I started to keep a log of Altman moments. One occurred at a rock show I was working. Lazing around in the crew room, I tossed a full bottle of confiscated booze into a cart loaded with similar bottles, and mine (shockingly) exploded when it hit the heap. It sent glass and Boone's Farm Apple Wine and Ripple and MD (Mad Dog) 20/20 flying up onto Dick Bonninger, boss of the two hundred security guys and former Green Beret who'd done thirteen months in Vietnam. When the mess hit him, Dick did a squirming, save-me-from-the-cooties dance, a jumping fuss and fidget. Dick was smaller than I was, but a fierce Irish terrier sort of guy. I'd seen him in action a few times, and though I didn't think he had murder in him—not anymore—he surely had something close. Dick's look across all the confiscated booze said something very surprising, though: *Wipe all this from your memory, OK? Forget about the dance. And in return I won't do the Green Beret windpipe crack on you.* But *Please*—mostly what Dick was saying was *Please*. It was, in its way, a very tender moment.

Maybe it was a little like the moment that the two gamblers, played by Elliott Gould and George Segal, share in *California Split* when they break into a song-and-dance routine. "Rustus, Rastas, Johnson Brown," goes the chorus. "What you gonna do when the rent comes round?" With it, they do a sweetly maladroit soft-shoe. At any moment, one could have stopped and cracked up at the other's ridiculous blackface routine. But neither does: tenderly, wisely, they indulge each other.

Part of what made me love Altman was that he was against bigness. He always wanted to turn the carpet over. He wanted you to see the signs of strain and stress that went into the making of what looked like a serene, well-balanced thing. But he didn't want to debunk the whole show; he simply wanted to marvel at the quirky congestion of the threads. It was probably tough for the actors who played in his movies to redeem their Hollywood standing. He turned his stars into handheld sparklers. He waved them around. But he did it without resentment, without meanness: he simply liked them better that way. After Altman was through shrinking Warren Beatty in *McCabe and Mrs. Miller*, Beatty must have needed extended hours in his hotel suite, lined everywhere with mirrors, to bring his consolidated superstar self back into being. As Jacques Lacan tells us, without mirrors identity would forever be in danger of fracturing into a million bits. In the mirror we appear to be One.

All that I was learning from Altman, or thought I was, all the pleasure I was getting from seeing his movies, was at pretty radical variance with my job quest, which was not going well. Helena kept calling with interview prospects, but I kept telling her that I had prior engagements—often at the movies. (It turned out that you needed to see an Altman movie at least two or three times consecutively, then go back and catch it once or twice more.) But finally I'd have to say yes, and so I'd end up sitting in the office of this or that editor somewhere downtown. Once I almost succeeded in getting one of these jobs, only saving myself at the last moment.

The interview was for a job at a sailing magazine. I had actually spent time on a sailboat and knew stem from stern and port from starboard and the rest. A rich and generous friend at Bennington owned two or three boats and somehow got me on board one of them. ("Ah, sailing," she whispered as we walked across the commons lawn to dinner. She jutted her chin forward and closed her eyes and imagined she was being washed by salt-laden breezes.) Things seemed to be going well at the interview. The editor, a pockmarked woman with short hair and hanging earrings that played a welcoming symphony as she nodded her head up and down, encouraging me, asked if I had proofreading skills. I said that I did. This was a radical lie.

We were getting ready to close the deal when she asked me what the book was that I had in the pocket of my leather bomber's jacket. I flourished it, sure she would be interested. The book was Hegel's *Phenomenology of Mind*, given to me by Duggan as a Christmas present. I was pining for that book, in part because I knew that Hegel was Marx's big influence, that Pelops knew nothing about Hegel, and that I could use my Hegelian insight to cut Pelops off at the knees during our next installment of dialectical war. But the editor frowned; her intricate earrings stopped making the welcoming symphony, and I could see that I had blown the interview. (You can imagine what Senior said when I mentioned to him the part about flourishing the book.) But really, getting the job—despite the fact that I was a touch miserable without one—would have cut into my moviegoing time, my wandering-around time, my time doing nothing at all.

Pelops, predictably, didn't approve of my movie obsession. "If you want amusement, Homer," he said, "you only need to hit the street with me." There was truth in this. Going around with Pelops produced memorable encounters.

One night we dropped in on a friend of his, an astonishingly smart woman given to baggy, flowered dresses. Unbeknownst to Pelops, there was a party in process at her house. (Why hadn't Pelops been invited? Why hadn't I?) The door was open. In the front hall was a dish of brownies. I was hungry. Pelops was hungry. Ah, the thick, oozy chocolate in those brownies. But there was something grainy, a little mildewed in the taste. Pelops, who had been avoiding parties, stayed quite a while to talk to a young woman who was a roommate of his friend. She was extremely nearsighted yet refused to wear her glasses and so peered up with saintly mildness at Pelops.

"Homer," he said when we were back on Broadway, walking north, "wouldn't it be good to have a girlfriend who didn't see all that well? I mean, she's *soooo* unthreatening."

I found this remark easily the funniest utterance ever to pass human lips. I replayed it in my head. That last sentence about the girl's being so unthreatening, it turned out, was a sequence of words, and each word was like a plane on a many-sided cube. Each plane was uproariously funny in itself, and hilarious in the way that it contributed to the whole. I turned the cube over and over. I contemplated each amusing face: I laughed. In not too long, I was leaning against a mailbox, laughing as though I was being tickled by the forefinger of an invisible god.

Pelops had eaten fewer brownies than I had, but enough to bring on song. While I shook and squirmed, Pelops sang "Expressway to Your Heart" by the Soul Survivors.

Passers-by saw a giant, crooning with a Motown inflection, his eyes closed, and a bearded guy having what was as close as he'd come in some time to a religious experience. There were stares, guffaws, held noses. Pelops sang on. Other Motown hits followed. At one point, Pelops launched into a number with one verse: "Do the monkey dance." As he sang it over and over, he executed the dance, rolling his forearms over each other in a treadmill motion and slinging his body salaciously from side to side. "Do the monkey dance!" And also "Doooooo the monkey dance!" And, with elision, "DotheMonkeyDance!"

This lasted for an indeterminable period of time. Then Pelops more or less carried me to the subway. Why, with access to experiences like this, did I need movies?

But in time, I scored myself yet another moviemaking idol. This was Woody Allen, whom I occasionally saw speed walking up and down Fifth Avenue. He wore a soft, explorer-type jungle hat, and stared intently at the ground, as if expecting that at any moment, it might insult him. Occasionally (yes, I followed him—one step of mine equal to his two), he peeked up to see if he was being peeked at. Then he looked down and did the ant walk again, linear, purposive, and tense. You half imagined that he had antennae under the hat, and that he was taking instructions in formic.

I watched all of his movies, seeing them multiple times, getting to the point where I could recite five-minute swatches of his dialogue with no problem. (This may have been an inherited gift, since my father had a similar capacity. He could run *The Maltese Falcon* almost from end to end.) So in time I saw *Sleeper, Everything You Always Wanted to Know About Sex, Love and Death, Bananas, Take the Money and Run*, and *Annie Hall*. Woody seemed to feel that identity, male identity in particular, crystallized in about 1956—let's say on April 7, at four in the afternoon. Men want what they want. They're perpetually horny. They always need to get laid—and usually no one's willing. But occasionally, through sheer luck, a volunteer steps forward. What happens then? The guy doesn't want her. (The rejection of the beautiful Allison Porchnick in *Annie Hall* is as plangent a scene as Woody ever played.) It's the girl across the street or down the block or the one roving around in his fantasies that he has to have. She'll truly make him happy; she'll get him to stop wanting. (What is a romantic? Nietzsche asks. It's a person who always wants to be elsewhere.) Woody is a wind-up toy powered by need (*desire* is too refined a term), but he's a self-aware wind-up. He's hip to the comedy of his endless and absurd wants. Not being able to get any satisfaction isn't tragic, or even something to inspire rock-and-roll grandeur, juiced by power chords from Keith. It's simply the male lot in life.

As to women's lot, who knows what that is? Women are what Woody's Viennese foster father called them, the Dark Continent. Only one thing about them is certain: they add more frustration to an already frustrating game. Woody wants respect, power, money, a better apartment, more money. But all these wants collapse into, and are shaped by, the one great want, the sex want. Women only make this commodity available when you don't care to have it, then they insist, insist, insist, and finally grow furious. When Woody visits the future in *Sleeper*, he learns that science has discovered beyond doubt that men and women are incompatible, erotically and in every other way, too. Everyone finally knows as much and acts accordingly. Want sex? Climb into the Orgasmatron. Alone.

All the business about peace and love, about social conscience, about the brotherhood of man, the stopping of this or that war, all the terrain of cultural crises that Woody traverses, is shown to be, in the essential mind of the male, subsidiary to the one true crisis, the sex crisis. What is a political rally

87 •

to Woody? It's a place much like a museum or a gallery or a book party, where available women leave their sanctuaries and expose themselves as though on the savannah. Nothing has changed since 1956: women are still insanely desirable and weird; society is hypocritical; selfishness and double-dealing are everywhere. No one, least of all Woody, is an exception to this rule. He's in it for himself and will say or do most anything to get what he most desires, which once had turns out, of course, to be radically undesirable.

Woody was the great anti-1960s man. The idea that culture had burst forth with a banquet of pleasurable options, that you could do your own thing, create your own mind again, remake your nervous system (as Norman Mailer, monarch of the time, was fond of saying), experience new forms of joy—these things were part of the Aquarian legacy. And Woody obviously found them absurd. He clearly detested Bob Dylan, probably for being, despite depths and twists of irony, so hopeful about realizing the demands he made on the world. Dylan, always disillusioned, still desires; Woody's disillusioned all the time, and comes back because that's all you can do: human beings are walking repetition compulsions.

During those pavement-scraping days, Woody was to me the great artist of disillusionment, doses of which I badly needed from time to time. Woody had succeeded, yes, he was a grand success. But part of what he told me, hyperbolically enough, was that success didn't bring frustration to an end. On the contrary, it may have even made matters worse. When you got the job, the loft, and the salary, you believed that life owed you yet more satisfaction—a decent love life, good friends, an occasional dose of inner tranquillity. You took it as an affront when the gods didn't deliver these things. Who the hell were they to stiff you? But Woody told me differently. Make all the money you want, get the golden job: the only thing that desire for stuff outside yourself's going to get you is more desire, and desire hurts.

My desires for sex and romance and more tender companionship than what Pelops could offer weren't getting much satisfaction. When I moved into the apartment, Pelops had guaranteed a life of teeming erotic bliss: he claimed that it went with the rock-and-roll-job persona that I was about to put on. But the backstage scene where I spent my time was about as tightly hierarchical as the court of Louis XIV. The groupies and the party girls thought it well beneath them to consort with the grunts who threw the amps around. The women I met in my cab were—well, they were the sort of women who took cabs. They seemed rich and fussy to me, not my type at all. So it wasn't a bad thing to have Woody around to suggest to me that Eros could often be—maybe always was—another of the world's glowing illusions.

It was during my Woody obsession that I had an interview at *Newsweek*. This was the big one, for I was talking to the boss, or the primary sub-boss, or something. I got myself a haircut; I even trimmed my beard a little. ("The hair shows that you can play by the rules; the beard shows creativity," said Duggan. "You look awful," said Pelops.) I borrowed a suit from Duggan, which somehow fit me splendidly. The night before the interview, I peacocked up and down East Eighty-sixth Street with Senior and Duggan, a copy of the *New York Times* under my arm. I'd even put my jangling cab change into a paper bag, brought it to the bank, and with the resulting paper bought myself a pair of brown lace-up shoes. The leather whimpered softly as I walked. "You are a suit man," said Senior with great satisfaction.

Again, the interview was going splendidly. The editor sat in a vast room, dominated by red—the court of the Crimson King, I thought, remembering the rock song. The Crimson King wanted to talk about what it was like going to a girls' college (I told him it was good); he wanted to talk about where Helena would be spending the weekends over the summer (the Hamptons, I thought); but finally he took an interest in me and my possible affiliation with his magazine. He asked if I had been on my school newspaper. I hadn't, but then there had been no newspaper. (Not only had there been no newspaper at Bennington, there was also no school song, no school colors, no football team, no fraternities, no sororities: the place seemed to be dedicated, in about equal degrees, to the arts and to sexual intercourse.) He asked me if I liked a bunch of novels that he seemed to like and I told him more or less that I did. I asked if he was writing a novel. This was the correct question. Maybe he was, maybe he wasn't. A lot of people in New York, he told me, were interested in the answer to my question. If he were writing a novel, he asked, what did I think it would be about? What was my guess? I picked something Hemingway-like, involving bulls and fishes. King Crimson—my monarch of the moment—smiled contentedly. All was going well.

But then it occurred to me that I hated *Newsweek* magazine. Something about its style, which was sycophantic and superior at the same time, made me slightly ill. In fact, Duggan and I had recently collaborated on an essay about *Newsweek* and *Time*. We'd borrowed some terms and attitude from Roland Barthes's *Mythologies* and we'd indicted the mags for being modern mythmakers, "sources of slick, palatable entertainment." I decided that the boss had to know about this paper. I described it at some length. I also told him about Roland Barthes and where he might like to start reading in the Frenchman's oeuvre. Now the monarch was truly excited. He loved this. He loved me. He deeply enjoyed the way I was attempting, using my undergrad tools, to dismantle the castle of illusion he lived in and that was his base for traveling to the Hamptons and chasing after Helena and trying, maybe, to effect the literary miracle of the bulls and the fishes.

It took me the length of three subway rides—the number I had to take to get from his downtown court to 187th Street—to recognize that I'd blown the interview completely. I had no chance for the job, and King Crimson was going to give Helena such an earful that I'd probably never get another interview in publishing. For a while I was disconsolate. I felt like taking the new shoes I'd bought for the interview, placing them neatly on the concrete porch at 187th Street, and setting them on fire. I would sit cross-legged beside them watching them burn. But in another province of my soul—the one that Woody had colonized, or maybe created—I was relieved. Maybe I was even happy. Success begets desire, which begets more desire, and desire—well, you know what that is: "Ah me! alas, pain, pain ever, forever," as the poet says.

So I cut myself loose from the job quest and once again took up my cab driving and my amp stacking and my Altman-inspired rambling, where the only rule was to look, but not to want—because you can't really want anything and see it at the same time. I became again a tripper around the great city, strolling here and there, an aristocratic bum. I stopped wanting and needing the conventional stuff. The desire for the great good thing was alive somewhere inside me, but for a while, there in dirty, fascinating New York, even that desire rested.

Better even than Woody, Lord Schopenhauer understands the suffering imposed by desire. But unlike Woody, Schopenhauer has a solution: We can consider things without interest, without wanting. We can suspend desire. We can do all we can to observe life calmly. "It is the painless state prized by Epicurus as the highest good and as the state of the gods," the philosopher says. "For that moment we are delivered from the miserable pressure of the will. We celebrate the Sabbath of the penal servitude of willing." After that day in King Crimson's throne room, I was a little more at peace, a little calmer. And though that state couldn't last—given my questing nature, how could it?—I prized it while I had it and, looking back, I prize it still.

4

LIFE DRUGS, DEATH DRUGS

(consciousness)

One fall day, by special invitation, I made the trip downtown to visit with Duggan Senior, my capitalist Socrates. It was early in the afternoon, a Saturday, and Senior was in what I'd come to think of as his cockpit, installed at his kitchen table, buffed and decked in gold and sipping from a vat-size red plastic cup of coffee, with Duggan beside him. I sat down, Senior and I began to chat, and in time it became clear that something or other was in the offing for Duggan and me—a piece of our education, no doubt. "You may catch something interesting today," he said. But Senior wasn't letting on what it was to be. I looked around the kitchen, with its blinding silver appliances and virgin butcher board, and glanced at Duggan, who was studying the *New York Times*—Duggan spent about two hours a day immersed in the newspaper; he descended into it like a diver dropping beneath the surface—and then looked back at Senior, trying to imagine what was up: no dice.

By now I'd spent plenty of time with Senior, mostly with Duggan there but occasionally not, listening to him reflect on many things—his interests were varied—but chiefly on two prime subjects, the glories of capitalism and the glories of coffee. We spent plenty of time sipping his brew and discussing how it might be made stronger—brought to the color of the onyx that sat at the center of one of his gold rings—using this new brewing process or that. Senior was forever hitting the street to buy new coffee-preparation devices, which usually looked like miniature spacecraft, each designed by a slightly different alien culture. Late on Friday afternoons, Senior got off the subway by East Eighty-sixth Street, the commercial strip nearest his apartment, and cruised up and down visiting the retail outlets. He bargained like a Bedouin with the owners, talked them past their profit margins, then a few dollars into their wholesale cost. But he made it up to them by giving them tips on how to improve their businesses. By about nine o'clock, he was back home with an enormous pile of goods, often including a new coffee module.

If Duggan and I were driving our cabs on a Friday night, we would stop by the apartment. The doormen loved the idea that they had a cabdriver living on the eleventh floor of a Park Avenue luxury building, and they sometimes reserved two spaces in front for our cartoon-yellow rigs. (The residents hated this and complained, but the doormen, who were in fact Dominicans and did like baseball and loved Duggan and Duggan Senior, affected not to understand.) We'd sit with Senior for an hour or so, drinking his imperial brew, as he rhapsodized about free markets, good stuff to buy, and the freedom to do what you hoped to do in the world, as well as—this part was pointed especially at me after my job-search debacles—how to get that freedom and not lose it. Twenty minutes before it was time to go, Senior would call down to the doorman, who'd start soliciting residents as they came out of the apartment to see if they needed a cab. The idea was to find top-price jobs, airport runs if possible. When we arrived at street level, we often had fares sitting in our cabs, waiting.

But this Saturday afternoon was a noncab day: I'd been summoned, so I'd risen early—a little before noon—and ridden the subway downtown. I kept looking and blinking, blinking and looking. Something was in the offing. Duggan kept reading the paper. Senior kept musing on one matter and another.

The doorbell rang; Senior rose to answer it. Duggan raised his head from the *Times*; he particularly loved today's edition, the Saturday, as well as the Monday. Those were the editions, I learned, where the fat and gristle—all the entertainment and lifestyle coverage—were cut away and the paper went hardcore news. Reluctantly, Duggan put the *Times* aside and led me into an alcove off the living room, which today was full of raging autumn sunlight. There about to be seated were Senior's guests, three businessmen wearing suits on a Saturday. They were younger than Senior, and two of them were keeping it mellow with paisley ties and hockey-stick sideburns.

"I'm sitting down to hear what you have to say," Senior told the three buddies; "the boys"—he pointed to Duggan and me—"are here for some education." The trio had a proposition for Senior, and they proposed it—God, did they propose it. They pitched him up and down and sideways. They pulled

95 •

CHAPTER 4 : LIFE DRUGS, DEATH DRUGS (CONSCIOUSNESS)

out charts; they punched calculators; they made their pencils dance on their legal pads. They wanted Senior to invest; they offered projections about his share of the profits. They offered enticing prospects.

Then they paused for Senior's reaction. But Senior said nothing. He did not speak a word. They continued to pitch; they continued to pose questions. Yet no matter what they said or asked, they could not get an utterance out of him. At one point, the desert of silence he created was so long and dry and unnerving that it began to take physical form in my imagination. The sand was industrial brown; the ground was strewn with the carcasses of beasts wasted in their attempted treks through; the sky was smeared ink; a noxious wind blew sand grains around like tiny bullets. I was ready to jump in—any utterance would have been a wash of spring rain. But as I was about to speak, Duggan tapped my foot beneath the table. I kept quiet and continued to sip my cup of carbon black, my third cup of the day, counting the installment of Dominican I'd made on 187th Street.

The trio members became desperate. They began to perspire. They recharacterized the investment idea in terms that seemed ever more favorable to Senior. Still he said nothing. He simply looked at them with an expression that indicated two things: that he did not fully believe what they were saying but that nonetheless he rather liked them as human beings. They began asking him more questions. One looked Senior in the eye and inquired into his view on the best place to acquire a certain sort of loan. Nothing. Senior would not speak. This went on for an hour, or what seemed like one. Then finally, at long last, Senior made his pronouncement. Word came from on high. "There's something about this transaction I don't understand," he said. Then he told them where his comprehension fell short. The three were so grateful for the words that they began tumbling over each other re-redescribing the deal in terms that even I could recognize as insanely favorable to Senior.

When the last peep was peeped and the last concession made, Senior, having told the fellas that he'd think their proposition over, showed them to the door with the greatest cordiality. Altogether, he had spoken no more than a hundred words.

When they were gone, he turned to me and Duggan. "That," he said with royal weariness, "was a lot of work." He glanced ceilingward and sighed a pasha's sigh. "I need a nap." He turned and disappeared into the Senior sanctum and left us standing outside in the hall to contemplate his performance. We'd just enjoyed a religious moment. Duggan and I had had a lesson in Zen capitalism.

Duggan let me know that he had to go back to his paper— the massive Sunday installment would be available at his newsstand in seven and a half hours, and he needed to be completely finished with the Saturday so as to be positioned for the sequel. I said good-bye, left the apartment, and trundled out of the building, off across Madison, then Fifth, and into Central Park.

The sun was laughing in the sky; the air was so clear and clean-seeming that it felt like an extra quotient of oxygen was coming into my lungs. Objects leapt toward me, bright and insistent, as though they'd been ever so lightly coated with ice; the trees ran mad with their fall colors. I was jittery from the coffee overdose, my hands trembling slightly like a perp's, and I had an odd taste in the back of my mouth, raw and a little sulfurous. My hyperalert state only seemed to enhance the bounty of the day.

Walking across the Sheep Meadow, I ran into a few people I knew from Bennington, and they were clearly in an elevated mood. As they approached, I saw one of them, the guy up front, half skipping. He was leading the others along, doing what seemed like a Pied Piper routine, inviting the multitude to come and join the dance. Already he had a mass of six or so. His name was Weston.

We exchanged greetings, while Weston's group jived in place behind him. He noticed that I was a little fidgety. (Was it that obvious?) I admitted I was and said something about ingesting too much of the carbon black. "Capitalist fuel," he said, "keeps the slave's engine running." I took this in, but before I could say any more, Weston reached into his pocket and pulled out a pellet. "Here," he said, "this will definitely mellow you out." It was such a small, small pill, how much could it do? I was getting way too squirrelly from the coffee. Why not take it? I looked at Weston's entourage, most of whom seemed to be dancing now to unheard and unhearable melodies. "C'mon, man," Weston said. "This will definitely even you out."

Is it possible that there was a time in America when it was impolite to refuse free drugs? Was there a time when it was an affront not only to the provider, but to the Woodstock Music and Arts Fair and the Grateful Dead and the peace sign not to take them? There *was* such a time, and though the time was passing on that screaming fall day, it had not disappeared entirely. I took the pill, and I swallowed it.

In the next half hour or so, strolling along beside Weston (I refused to get back into the pack and boogie), I came to understand that what I had suspected was true. I had ingested LSD, and I was about to see and feel strange things. Weston's coterie had done the same, and they were now in the process of evacuating conventional reality, perhaps for something better, perhaps not. I tried to pretend that we were off on a simple walk through the park; I tried to pretend that I wasn't scared at all. But I was terrified of LSD, and I had reason to be.

At Bennington I'd watched acid do its work on a guy named Billy Bonella. Billy was from Los Angeles, where his father was a well-to-do plastic surgeon. Billy was very non-Bennington. He was almost the only person in the place with an Italian surname and the only one capable of showing up at a party wearing gold jewelry dangling from his neck. He was a slight guy who looked like a composite of the members of Rod Stewart's rock group, Small Faces. Billy had an oblong face, a shag haircut, a little bit poodly, and a wry, agreeable expression. He had the pipe-cleaner arms of a slightly malnourished, born-during-the-Blitz Liverpool kid. When he arrived at Bennington, where drugs were radically unfashionable, he probably didn't have much of a history with them. Where he got the acid he did on that Friday night I'm not sure, but it was clearly his first time tripping.

At around nine o'clock, Billy came to my dorm room, where I was sitting around with my friend Robby, a guy who hung out at the college, though he actually wasn't enrolled. We were trying to figure out the "Wandering Rocks" chapter of *Ulysses*. We were also trying to hatch the first line for a brochure about the college that the admissions office had hired me to compose—it had to be written from a student perspective. I'd had the project for three months and couldn't come up with anything, so I brought on Robby as a collaborator. He couldn't think of any really marvelous first sentence either, though both of us felt sure that the sentence had to be splendid beyond human comprehension.

There was no knock that I heard. My door boomed open. In front of us was Billy, looking as though he was surrounded by a swarm of ghosts. He was sweating and his sweat smelled badly of fear; his eyes looked like brown marbles ready to pop out of his face. Well behind him were two guys I knew pretty well, who, it turned out, had been serving as Billy's minders for the last three hours. They'd seen my light on, and they'd come upstairs. They told us that Billy had taken acid, that he was doing strange things, that they were exhausted, and that Robby and I, like it or not, were now in charge of him.

What had Billy been up to that night? we asked the minders before they left. Many things. He had played an electric guitar—though Billy did not, could not, play electric guitar. He had run about twenty laps around the Commons building, his two minders following closely. During the last few laps, he had removed items of clothing and tossed them behind him.

He had been talking all night, often incoherently. Did he know where he was? Sometimes. Did he know his own name? Yes. As he entered the dorm room where Robby and I were alternately applying the theories of Wolfgang Iser to Joyce and laying impotent siege to the virgin sheet of paper rolled into my typewriter, Billy was in midconversation with no one in particular. The subject was "It."

"I want it," said Billy. "I've got to have it."

"What is *it*?" one of the minders asked. When he did, Billy gave him a look of high exasperation. What an absurd question! Yet it soon turned out that Billy himself did not know what *it* was, though he was willing to entertain conjectures.

"Is it sex?"

"That's not it," he replied.

"Is it food?"

"That's not it."

"Is it God?"

This one drew an especially derisive reaction: "That's *really* not it." But generally, Billy's dismissals of our candidates—for Robby and I got into the game quickly—were flat, low-key, and rather ducal. In the past, Billy had occasionally mentioned that he hoped to become a rock star and now, like a rock star, he wanted everything done for him, including, it seemed, his thinking.

I was stumped. I didn't know whether to shoot high or low. I couldn't say whether the *it* in question was something as simple as a new pair of underwear or the Gnostic key to the universe. We kept lobbing the ball over the net—job, home, his father the doc, his two brothers, his dog (Callahan by name)—and Billy kept sending them back with a maddeningly unbeatable topspin. What was *it*?

After a while, only Robby and Billy and I were left playing the *it* game, sitting on the bed in my second-floor dorm room, across from an open window covered with a screen, letting the breeze blow through. "That's not it." "That's not it." Billy said this over and over, even while Robby and I were silent. Apparently, when we weren't providing candidates, Billy was coming up with his own, internally. But he seemed to be shooting them out of his mental sky, one by one, like a marksman plugging skeet. "That's not it." "That's not."

I stood up and went to my closet to grab something or other; there was a mirror inside its door.

Billy edged Robby out of the way, got up off the bed where he was sitting, and pressed his face within a half inch of his reflection. He ran his hand through his Small Faces shag and stared. "I gotta tell you something," he said. "I got news for you guys."

I imagined, and I expect that Robby did, too, that we were finally going to find out what *it* was.

The next thing was said softly, but with intense conviction. "My head is shrinking."

"What?" This came from me and Robby at more or less the same time.

"My head. It's getting smaller."

He was serious. He believed it. Robby and I denied the hypothesis. We told Billy that his head was in the same fine proportion to his body that it always had been. Billy had the evidence of his own drug-enhanced vision to go on, though. "Fuck no. It's shrunk. And it's getting smaller all the time."

Ridiculous! Absurd! But I kept staring at Billy and something odd began to happen. His head did seem smaller: not a lot, at least not at first, but as the seconds clicked off on their way to eternity or wherever they go, I saw a change. In not too long, Billy's head was going to look like one of those purple-black rubber heads with the drooping eyes and hanging nether lips that people in my high school suspended from the rearview mirrors of their Pontiac Trans Ams, with the Hooker headers and the hemis and the spoilers.

Billy persisted. He was sure that his head was getting smaller. He sat down again on the bed but it was clear he was beginning to panic. "Jesus, what am I going to tell my mother?" At one point, the nadir of our support effort, Robby turned to me and whispered—loud enough, alas, for Billy to hear—"You know, his head really does look a little bit smaller than it was. Not that much. But a little."

Billy, hearing this, said, "Pretty soon my head's going to be the size of a baseball. Billy 'Baseball Head' Bonella, that's what they're gonna call me." And Billy's head—I was sure of it now—*was* getting smaller. Robby and I put our (presumably normal-size) heads together. We had to figure out what to do. While we strategized, Billy entered a new area of reflection.

"Birds fly," Billy said. "Birds fly. Airplanes fly. Insects fly. To fly. Really. To fly."

Robby and I thought that he was composing an acid haiku, up here on the second floor of my Bennington dorm. "To fly," Billy said proudly. It was as though he had invented not only the concept of flight but the words to express it. He pronounced the words as though he could taste them, and they tasted like cream of an unbelievably subtle and rich sort.

Slowly, almost decorously, Billy rose from the bed, leaned forward, and took a step. Very quickly he accelerated. He propelled himself straight on, bent at the waist, as though he was going to use his fast-shrinking but still rock-solid head to blow the screen out of the window and then take off. He took another stride, another. It was a long way down, and it was not going to end well. Robby and I went for him. I came in high and hard; Robby took his feet out. It was a deep, solid, satisfying tackle, better than most any I'd made as an inside linebacker for the Medford Mustangs a few years before. We lay there for a while in a lump, limbs everywhere like a congress of worms. "Bill," Robby said, "I think that we're going to have to go down to the first floor."

• •

Billy was on my mind that day in Central Park. He, too, had been a quester after that gorgeous elusive entity, *it*. Like me, Billy had been searching for the great good thing. And look what it had done to him. Was I going to follow him once that little pill kicked in? Who would be there to catch me if I did?

At the start, I was anything but tranquil—Billy's story, along with my coffee overdose and the jitters acid brings in the early stages, all saw to that. But I was in an autumn paradise: The air was a celebration; the sun was a gentle monarch. It was one of those rare New York days when everyone seems to be in a good mood.

As the acid began taking hold—colors brightening, sounds deepening—I felt myself grow calmer. The day was simply too wondrous for me, or probably anyone else, to go off the edge and into free-fall. When the colors and textures around me reached full intensity—I was seeing, it struck me, the way certain painters must see all the time—and every sound seemed to echo gorgeously off the vault of the sky, I peeled away from Weston's group and began to wander, drinking in the noise and the colors and the passing people, who all seemed more distinctive and vital somehow, more emphatically themselves. My vision was so sharp: it was as though someone had suddenly cleaned the interior glass, cleaned the windshield. I'd had no idea that it had gotten so dense with grime. (LSD: the ultimate squeegee man.) Songs from radios and boom boxes crisscrossed each other in the air and threaded together into sweet hybrid tapestries of sound. The breeze washed over me like unseen water. Finally I plunked myself down on the top of a small hill. In front of me, dominating the field, was an oak tree in its full flush of autumn color.

The tree, it seemed, was burning. It was a grand red, gold, and orange torch flaming against the sky. I sat amazed by it, the way a child sits staring delighted into a campfire or a grown man or woman stands thrilled and a little afraid in front of an empty warehouse going up in flames. But the tree wasn't only burning. The tree, I saw, was breathing, too. It expanded and contracted in a smooth rhythm. It swelled up and drew in, peaceful and confident, in steady time—a giant kingly form, it seemed to me, preternaturally composed, clothed all in fire.

Soon the tree and I were breathing together. We inhaled and sent air out simultaneously. In and out, in and out, in and out: calm and large and slow the breaths came. We were connected. We were both alive, this great, sheltering god and I. I looked away from the tree for a moment, at the shrubs and bushes and the grass—the grass that rolled out like an inviting carpet before me and the intricate blades that created a tiny jungle around my feet. And those things, too, emitted vital breath. All nature was alive. (How had I never seen this before? I had heard it said—I had known it. But I had never *seen* it.) All things, humans and animals and green plants, were breathing and together composed a giant being. I was part of all this, too: I was at home here.

My hands weren't trembling anymore, and the sulfurous taste had left my mouth. I thought of Billy and what he'd suffered that night, and I wished that he could have seen this rather than whatever it was that launched him toward my window. I wanted him to experience this wonder: I wanted everyone to.

"This is all me and I am all this," I said to myself as I stared across the park. And in this I included people who, walking down the streets in the soft rage of rush hour, could seem

CHAPTER 4 : LIFE DRUGS, DEATH DRUGS (CONSCIOUSNESS)

like so many distinct warring individuals, who wanted me and most of the others they shared the city and earth with to get out of their way. In that everyday world, humans were obstacles to each other. But really we were part of a single being. Now maybe I could walk down the street, look at each person I passed, and think, "Yes, yes, that is me, too. We're no different. We're one and the same."

It was obvious to me now why the Buddhists revered all living beings and why Jains—whom I had once thought to be slightly deranged—sometimes insisted on going through life veiled so as to do no harm to the tiny creatures who might fly into their eyes and noses and be snuffed out. They didn't want to destroy any part of the miracle. The beautiful Isha Upanishad, one of the sacred texts of the Hindus, puts it this way:

Those who see all creatures in themselves
And themselves in all creatures know no fear.
Those who see all creatures in themselves
And themselves in all creatures know no grief.
How can the multiplicity of life
Delude the one who sees its unity?

This "One Life," as the poet and opium devotee Coleridge called it, was, I felt, surpassingly vulnerable. It had to be taken care of, because there were many forces arrayed against it: technological forces, forces of civilization, and the force of human obliviousness.

I had been sitting for so long that when I tried to stir my legs, they were stiff as the Tin Woodsman's. I must have creaked as I pushed myself up and finally stood. But still, I couldn't leave the spot. I couldn't stop staring at that tree, flaming away against the sky, a benevolent dragon, covered in jewel-like scales: red, orange, yellow, gold.

This "one life within us and abroad" was tender, I saw, flowerlike. But it had something fierce in it, too. That tree had a hunger for being. It wanted to enlarge and grow: it wanted to spawn more trees and more. As tender as it was, the tree was ravenous for life, and even as I felt the fragility of natural things, I felt their furor, too. If we bombed our planet into gray dust, I thought, still, in time, a thousand years or a million, a green shoot would push its way through the radio-active loam with a life as vulnerable and fierce as the life of the great tree burning and breathing in front of me.

"All of this is here, all of the time," I said to myself. "It's all here all of the time. You can have it whenever you want it." All that I was experiencing could be present without the drug as well as with it, I thought. I was penetrating to a constantly present world. "You can have it when you want it," I told myself again.

I stretched and looked up into the sky. What time was it? Had an hour gone by since I'd reached the hill, or two or three? By the looks of the sun, I might have been here for a long time. I began to walk down into the park toward the zoo, and as I did, I felt a shiver of fear hit me. Could I really get this sort of feeling back when I wanted it? Maybe my way of being day-to-day set me apart from this One Life that I felt I was touching.

"How do you know," asks Blake, "but ev'ry Bird that cuts the airy way / Is an immense world of delight, clos'd by your senses five?" The beauty's out there all the time, the poet suggests, only we can't perceive it. For if we saw too much, felt too much, enjoyed too much, we might stop performing.

We wouldn't be productive. The social engine that we're a part of would cough and stutter. So down go the gates that block full perception—*ka-blam!*—like the metal awnings that the shopkeepers slam closed at the end of the day to protect their holdings. Would I ever be able to lift those doors up again, reopen my five senses? And when you do reopen your senses—if you can—then what kind of fate befalls you? What gains are possible? What losses?

To fly. That afternoon, sitting on the hill, contemplating my tree, I'd felt myself propelled into an inner space of knowing. I yearned to go beyond appearances, get it all. Figuratively, I'd wanted to fly—and maybe I had. Billy Bonella had something more literal in mind. If Billy had died that night at Bennington—and the fall from my second-floor dorm room could have killed him—would he have been a casualty in the one true battle, the one that Blake and other visionaries all the way back to the Upanishads fought, the battle for the expansion of the mind? Naturally I'm interested in drugs, William S. Burroughs once said. As a writer, I'm interested in anything that enlarges consciousness, my own and other people's. How could I not be interested in drugs?

But drugs can be like wolves: they pick out the weaker ones from the fold and take them down. The way a heroin addiction or a craving for methamphetamine can tear first the child, then his family to pieces—put a mother, in particular, through earthly hell—is a horror not easy to match. One of my college roommates, a devoted pothead, began by sitting on his bed, smoking weed, and rocking back and forth to Jethro Tull. Then he began sitting on the bed with the lights out, rocking back and forth without Jethro Tull. What happened to him? One day he had to leave, and he never came back.

The word on this was simple—he "flipped out": "Johnny Crow? Oh yeah, he flipped out and had to go home."

Should we insist on and ingest more drugs, better drugs, knowing that our less resilient or less lucky brothers and sisters are likely to find those drugs—or be found by them—and go down? Shall we keep the drug culture alive, knowing that however strong we might feel today, when the wind comes on hard, or when it comes softly from a certain direction, we'll shudder ourselves and maybe fall?

Yet we still do not know who and what we are. We do not know what a mind is or what it might be able to achieve. We do not know with certainty what a good life is, or what justice is, or love. We have no conception of what worlds, if any, lie beyond this one. (Death remains what the prince called it: "the undiscover'd country from whose bourn / no traveler returns.") Any medium of discovery, be it words or music or paint or film or a chemical compound that promises to carry us beyond our current blinkered state, can never be blithely cast aside.

My friend Billy seemed to have been changed by his drug run. When I saw him afterward, he was still charming, still sweet, but he was diminished. (His head was, I can testify, at—or back to—original size.) He took up less karmic space; his aura was a sparrowlike gray-brown. But he and Coleridge and Burroughs and all the other drug visionaries—and myself, too—well, we had seen what we had seen.

In 1975, in New York and elsewhere, mind expansion was becoming less and less the name of the game. People turned to drugs not for enlightenment but for intensity. They sought more effective engagement with the world as it was: they were romancing the already given. In the music biz, I was in a position to see the changes up close.

One night, hoping to get out to work at Roosevelt Stadium—Alice Cooper was coming—I arranged a ride with a couple of security guys from Pelops's crew, guys I didn't know terribly well. Even if all went smoothly, if they picked me up on time and booted it over the bridge to Jersey, there was a chance I was going to be late. This wasn't something I could readily afford. Pelops and I had recently pissed Dave off, and I felt now that he was probably gunning for me, getting ready to toss me off the stage crew and back onto security, where I'd started.

Maybe he was right to be mad. A few days before, Pelops and I had played a particularly aggressive game of "find the phone." Pelops and I had no telephone: Pelops had gotten into a many-pronged dispute with the Ma Bell authorities, so no line for him. My credit record had a few flaws. The one time we did manage to get a phone installer on the scene, he saw the Patty Hearst poster and bolted. But Dave did have a phone: it was a gleaming red contraption, and it was paid for by our rock production company. The phone was off-limits to me and to Pelops, unless the situation was life or death. ("And what do you suppose could actually kill Junior here?" Dave asked of Pelops.) When Dave finished up his business for the day, he hid the phone to keep the two of us from racking up monster charges, or simply abusing the thing. The apartment was small, but Dave was excellent at hiding things.

Eventually we got to the point of using a tool to lift the parquet floor squares off, one by one. We found the phone, too, under the third floorboard square or so, and we'd made hay with it. I called an old girlfriend and tried to get her to come to New York for the Alice Cooper show. (Alice who?

No!) Pelops actually called his parents—and did not request funding. But as was to be expected, we did not cover our tracks well. So the next day, Dave rose at the crack of dawn (about eleven o'clock) and began orating. He aimed the invective at Pelops, who for some reason became insanely submissive when Dave rampaged, but it was clearly meant for me, too.

So I desperately did not want to be late for the Alice Cooper crew call. It took me all afternoon to arrange the ride—using the outdoor street phone on the corner of Broadway, which had clearly served as a urinal to three generations of outdoor dwellers. Finally, by promising to pay for gas, pay for oil, and remunerate whatever squeegee guys materialized on the way to Jersey, I got two new security guys, guys who'd be guarding the equipment after I and my fellow stage-crew members went to bed at about three in the morning, to promise to come and take me to the stadium.

They showed up late enough so that if they'd shot directly across the George Washington Bridge—naturally, I was paying the toll—and to Jersey City, I'd about make it in under the radar of Dave's wrath. The two security guys stopped in front of the apartment in a van so rattly it looked like it needed to be bound together across the roof and underneath with a dense piece of rope, the way half-busted boxes are when the post office finally delivers them to you. Both of the guys wore blue-jean jackets with black leather sleeves; both had long pigtails, braided tight as a mandarin's. One was blond and looked like a Viking who'd spent too much time in the mead hall, bringing the fabled horn to his lips; the other, the driver, was short, with a pencil goatee and a ratty hypersmart face.

When I stepped up to the van, the Viking rolled himself back into the cargo space and gestured to the front seat, the shotgun spot. I thought this to be a gesture of deference. (When I was in high school, I'd seen blood shed over who would be riding shotgun and who wouldn't.) Maybe I was being indulged because I was stage crew, the working aristocracy of the production company; or maybe because I was paying for the gas and the tolls and the tread wear on the tires. I didn't have much time to enjoy my status, though. Instead of heading to the bridge, the driver turned left onto Broadway and began moving downtown.

"We got a stop to make first," the driver said.

"A very profitable stop," the Viking whooped.

It turned out that they were heading downtown to an apartment not far from Duggan's to transact some business. "Sorry if it fucks you up, man," the driver said. "There's gonna be something in it for you, though."

I remonstrated a little, but it was clearly no use. They were eventually going to the stadium, and I'd just have to cruise along and make the best of it. But then, as we were barreling downtown, the guy in the back piped up. "Hey," he said to the driver, "we gotta tell him."

"No, no way."

"We got to." They struggled like this for five minutes, Tweedledee and Tweedledum in high disputation.

Finally the driver made the call. "Truth is, man," he said, "you gotta know. I mean, you're riding on top of twenty years. I mean, really, you're right on top of it." The Viking laughed as though Egil had entered the hall with another half-dozen horns of ale.

"It's going to snow hard," the Viking said.

"Big storm coming," his pal announced. "Snow on the Upper East Side."

After I'd been working at rock and roll for about six months, it began snowing and it didn't stop. Snow persisted without significant letup for the next year I was on the scene and then on into the future. It created a cold, cold mind-set for people, "a mind of winter." Cocaine—blow, powder, snow—made people more energetic, more alert, but it also made them madly detached. It made them self-preoccupied, enhancing what the philosopher liked to call the *principium individuationes*, the principle of individuality.

Coke induced people to home in on their desires, then set to work like demons fulfilling them. A raise? A new job? This girl? That guy? No problem—I can go after that. I and I and I. The drug was all about self, and self versus others in particular. It built up the borders of the individual in the way that LSD and meditation and the Upanishads could—maybe—melt them down.

Cokeheads often did their drug in private. But when they got together, they engaged in a ritual that spoke volumes. Coke had to be snorted from a flat surface, and usually that was a mirror. It had to be drawn up the nose through a tube, almost always a piece of currency, a crisp hundred-dollar bill if possible. The partakers passed the bill around the circle, nodding somberly to each other in turn, affirming their fealty to the new gods, money and blow. They passed the hundred ritually from hand to hand. Money, which could in a moment be converted to more blow, was the new Eucharist. (They could just as well have used a rolled-up piece of notepaper.) Money was what united all—and when they looked down into the mirror to snort their lines, what they saw, aptly enough, was their own face, separate, looming, and distorted with desire. "One must have a mind of winter . . . ," Stevens says, "not to think / Of any misery in the sound of the wind, / In the sound of a few leaves. . . ." The not-thinking part, the not-feeling part, was the key.

During my last six months working at rock, coke was everywhere. Stage-crew members and security guys got all they could. At the end of the night, when the checks came out, the dealers stood at the end of the pay line, getting the money signed over. Many on the rock crews wore tiny silver spoons around their necks, sometimes ornately designed. They seemed almost like beggar's bowls, these spoons: the devotee signified his need by wearing them, much as the Buddhist monk signifies the need for alms and scraps of food with his wooden bowl. The rock scene was full of coke mendicants, always begging for a hit—a mind of winter, a head full of snow.

Coke was a class-creating drug, not, as pot often was, a class-dissolving one. There were those who had it and those who didn't, those who could afford it and those who couldn't. There were those invited into the bathroom for a hit, sometimes from off the top of a toilet of dubious cleanliness, and there were those locked outside. Coke was something people laid on superiors and on stars, on figures they wanted to impress or hoped to hang out with. Coke was the sacrificial offering of the day, what burnt thigh bones had been a few millennia before. It was what the reigning deities liked. When they got some, they often showed their approval with a snort and then a grunt. They accepted the offering and called it good.

There was always a toke of pot to spare for anybody, no matter how uncool. There was even the hope that pot might make the unhip hip, as though by white magic. Pot, its advocates believed, was sometimes a miracle drug. "We need to get him stoned," the pot devotee would say of someone who seemed promising but was still wearing his brown lace-ups and reporting to work on time.

Fortunately for me, I was all but indifferent to coke. Coffee may wear down the stomach lining, jazz the blood pressure a little, and dispense a few headaches—but coke can burn down the house. Guys on the stage crew went riffing on about blow not being addictive, and maybe in some chemical sense it isn't. But a drug that can make you feel like a god—and like a god who bears no particular responsibility for the creatures around him—is likely to hold an attraction for some that fully equals chemical addiction to tobacco and opiates. Coke was about hierarchy. With the coming of the age of coke, people found out quickly what they were worth. Generally it was less than they'd imagined.

Now, rattling through Spanish Harlem, I was sitting in a van full of poison with a couple of guys greedy to unload it. I really did not want to have to figure out how to get from where we were, among the bodegas and tenements and all-day, all-night street sitters, to Roosevelt Stadium in Jersey. It was going to necessitate going on something called a PATH train. People from New York got on PATH trains and never returned, or so I believed. But ten or twenty years in jail? I really didn't have the time.

"Out," I hollered. "Let me out."

"There'd be something in it for you," the driver said.

"You still have to pay for the gas," his pal announced.

"Bullshit," I said.

"No, you really do," the driver intoned. We were now twenty miles per over the speed limit.

"No!" I yelped.

"You gotta pay," they said, more or less at once.

"Alright," I said finally. "Let me out." They pulled over on upper Park Ave, about ten blocks north of Duggan's; I gave them my ten bucks, dropped into the subway, and approached a map, scarred thick with graffiti, and began to figure out how I was ever going to get to Jersey.

The PATH train proved about as impossible as I'd imagined, and by the time I reached the stadium, the security guys were already there, kicked back in green lounge chairs, guarding the amplifiers, drinking Heinekens. They affected not to recognize me. For his part, Dave gave me a degree-two exasperation look, and I went off and began helping to unload a semi that looked to be about as long as a New York City block. Alice was doing something called his Welcome to My Nightmare tour, and the set included a supersize Gothic-style bed, on which Alice, the dreamer, was to dream his terrifying dreams. There were two giant pillars to flank the bed, a giant spiderweb, and a giant spider to match. All of this and more we trundled off the truck and got into place for the night's extravaganza. Alice's roadies were about the best-spirited and most capable ones I'd met, but the night was still a grind. When the show, which I pretty much slept through, was finally over, we lined up to get paid outside the promoter's office. At the end of the pay line stood the backstage coke dealers, three of them, waiting to collect what was theirs.

5

HOW TO LEAVE NEW YORK

(nature)

One night, late in winter, Pelops and I were lounging around
the apartment on 187th Street engaged in debate. The subject this time wasn't my regressive bourgeois tendencies. The
terms of exchange were simpler. We were arguing about
whether it was possible to leave New York. Pelops claimed it
to be impossible. No one could leave New York City.

"Of course you can, Pelops," I told him. "You go to Port
Authority Bus Terminal, you purchase a ticket for somewhere, like Appleton, Wisconsin, or Bakersfield, California,
you get on the bus, and then, after a month or so, you get off
at the destination you paid for." I said this very slowly, fearing
as I did that Pelops had somehow altered his consciousness
through chanting or extended meditation.

"No, Homer," he told me. (It was never good news when

Pelops called me Homer. The name evoked my failed writing aspirations and was used when Pelops wanted to shrink me a size or two and enhance his own giant proportions.) "You must understand. If you were to buy such a bus ticket, you would indeed be driven hither and yon for a month and more. But then you would be dropped ignominiously in Queens, to make your way back to 187th Street, well behind on your rent."

"Really?"

"Yes," said Pelops, "and besides, as to Queens, I have it on excellent authority: the place does not exist."

"Pelops, your doctrine is false," I told him. Lenin, I'd learned in one of the books he foisted on me, used to march around Zurich during the two or so hours on Sunday afternoon that he gave himself for leisure each week, and as he marched he would sing his favorite song. The chorus ran: "Your doctrine is false. / Freedom can be fettered, but never permanently confined."

Pelops could see that I was low. I often hated driving the cab; I was tired of rock shows, even though Pelops would voice-over away at a hundred metaphors a minute to keep me entertained while we were working. New York was hopelessly grungy: there was now dismal third-rate graffiti on everything. Pelops said that he'd put his book bag down in the subway, begun reading, and looked up to see someone working out on the bag with a spray can. There was little clear surface available, and the scrawlers—and the artists, too—took what came their way. But now the scrawlers were way more numerous and fierce than the gifted practitioners.

It was so filthy everywhere that winter, that when I came back from a trip to buy newspapers—*Times* for me and Dave,

Post for Dave, *Daily Worker* for Pelops—I had a layer of Dickensian grime on my hands and face. I couldn't find a real job (not that I actually looked for one anymore), and I couldn't find a girlfriend. I was writing nothing. It was Pelops and me and Dave and the workers and the peasants.

I'd had my moment of illumination that day in Central Park, and I didn't doubt that what I'd learned about the One Life and the rest was true and probably enduring. But as to what to do with my knowledge, I had no real idea. It seemed foolish to go back to the well and drink the same water— try to bring on the vision again with another monster acid hit. I'd spent the two days following my park visitation in bed, and I felt like my imagination, such as it was, had been scorched. It was as though someone had chucked three sticks of dynamite into a small cave. The cave hadn't collapsed, but it was burnt, empty, and smoking. My writing drives seemed even more blocked up than usual: the checkpoints on the way to my forming a cogent sentence had enhanced security. Still, a basic question stayed with me: Once you knew—or thought you knew—that there truly was One Life in us and abroad, and that the life was both tender and fierce, what were you supposed to do? What kind of art could you make, what kind of work could you do, what kind of personal relations could you cultivate that would honor this knowledge?

Pelops sensed my desperation—for someone who could seem radically self-absorbed, he was astonishingly attuned to other people's emotional weather fronts—and he did what he could to find a remedy. What he was telling me that night when we debated leaving the city, I supposed, was that like it or not, New York is the center of the universe and anyone who leaves it voluntarily will always feel like he's flunked

Life 101: he couldn't hack it in the twenty or so square miles where reality is most intensely concentrated. He sent himself down to the minors. He faked an injury and hobbled off the field. Maybe Pelops was also telling me, in his Pelopsian way, that if I left town, he would miss me. Who else would listen to him as I would, ask him questions, read the books he stacked on my desk (or some of them), and join him for his weekly feast of chicken livers with peppers and onions?

Pelops sometimes seemed to feel that it was his revolutionary duty to monitor my mail, in part because my mother occasionally sent me shoe boxes full of brownies. Sometimes they did not reach their destination. "I had to protect you, Homer. I feared that they might have been laced with a mind-altering substance. You must remember your past experiences."

"Brownies from my mother?"

"Homer, one cannot be too careful."

"So you *dispatched* them?"

"They were strategically disarmed."

One day, not long after the discussion about whether it was or was not possible to leave New York, a piece of mail arrived that filled Pelops with concern. He handed it to me on a Saturday afternoon, at the top of the stairs; it was about two o'clock, and we'd both recently gotten out of bed. The letter had come first class—we almost never received a piece of first-class mail at 187th Street that was not a bill—and it was postmarked a week earlier. The return address, in official lettering, was the Outward Bound School in Boulder, Colorado. Outward Bound was—and is—a school that teaches people to get along in the wilderness and implants in them various outdoorsy values, or tries to. One day about three years before, hanging around at Bennington, I had, for no reason I could recall, sent them an application.

Pelops gave me his special hangdog look as he handed the letter over. He pulled his lower lip way down; he wrinkled his brows, hound style; he stared at the ground, and his mammoth glasses slid a quarter inch down his nose, making him look scholarly and discombobulated.

"I suspect this to be the end, Homer. But I wish it were not so."

The letter announced that I had been awarded a scholarship to the Colorado Outward Bound School, to participate in a course to begin late in the summer of that year. For a moment, my heart sang out. I could leave New York. I could cut loose.

"You would be missed, Homer, by me and by many," said Pelops, who had now given up any pretense of not knowing the contents of the letter.

But this sensitivity was transient. When Pelops saw that I wasn't immediately moved by his offering of affection, he began to declaim. He told me that if I left, I'd be responsible for the year's remainder of the rent; I'd have to find someone to take my room, someone who met with his approval; I'd have to clean said room; I'd have to clean the bathroom; I'd have to finish *Das Kapital* and answer a sequence of demanding but not unfair questions on it. The list continued.

I wasn't really sure I was going. I wasn't sure I wanted to go. I had no particular feeling about Outward Bound, other than that it was a thing that a lot of woodsy, hippie Bennington types did and claimed to love. It was a ticket out of New York; it was also free: they were even willing to pay my plane fare to Denver, Colorado, though not, for some reason, the fare back. And also, Pelops had in effect told me good-bye.

• •

But that wasn't quite my ultimate good-bye to Pelops and to New York: I actually found a more memorable way to quit the scene, or it found me. It turned out that rock and roll, wacky poltergeist that it was, had one more surprise left, and it was coming soon.

One cold night, out at the Capitol Theater in Passaic, after we'd loaded the amps into the truck, Dave called the stage crew all together. It was six or so weeks after my confab with Pelops on the subject of leaving New York, and I had virtually decided that I was going west. Dave informed us that he had amazing news. He had a spectacular gift to lay on us. We were going to be part of something astonishing, at least if we wanted to be.

Two months or so down the line, there was going to be a grand free concert, and it wasn't going to be here in the outback of New Jersey. No, the concert was going to take place in New York City, in Central Park—the place where I'd had my revelation. Every production outfit around had tried to get the gig, but we, the Schneider-Hamlin Group, had been selected. It was going to be our show.

"Who's going to play?" I asked.

"NeRPS," Dave said, meaning New Riders of the Purple Sage. "Or at least that's who everyone is going to think is playing."

"And they won't be?"

Dave looked at me with his fourth-degree exasperation look—he had about twenty valences. "They will be," Dave said. He blew invisible smoke out his mouth. "But it's who'll be playing with them that's incredible."

"Who?" asked Don Keller. Don was infatuated with Dave.

Some stage-crew guys and I had once approached him while he was stoned and begun asking him sincere questions about his commitment to Dave and to rock production. We asked him how high a building he'd be willing to leap from for Dave's sake. We'd started at one story and moved gradually up. At four you break both legs; at six you probably die. Don went to three.

Dave gave Don an industrial-strength version of the look he'd given me. "It will be amazing," he said, enunciating each word, as though he were counting out gold coins.

On a blowsy warm spring day six or so weeks later, I was to be found standing in a circle of people passing around a small white token of solidarity and lawlessness. We were in the Sheep Meadow back behind a stage that I'd spent about twelve hours helping to build the day before. I'd helped unload truck after truck—they kept rolling in—and by the time the amps were stacked, I was exhausted. I'd balled up my T-shirt, curled myself up behind an enormous sonic blasting machine, and gone to sleep. Now I was awake, and it was breakfast time, sort of—being well past noon—and because there were no sweet rolls to be found, I'd settled for a beer. Like almost everyone else there, I still did not know who the featured band was going to be. It was that big a secret. I knew, as everyone did, that New Riders of the Purple Sage were not going to be showing up and that only the monster group would be playing. Before I made my way to the circle, I'd ambled past the security guys and onto the corner of the stage. (I'd now been around the rock scene so long that I could actually *amble* past security guys—both a good thing and a not so good one.)

My ability to estimate human numbers has always been

second tier. I would have made a miserable general in the Napoleonic Wars, I suppose. But if I had to put forward a crowd estimate for that spring day, featuring a concert by a band unknown but presumed to be Big, I would have said that there were, give or take, 3 million people out there. Alright, maybe that's an overestimate; there were a helluva lot. I ambled (once more) wearily backstage and joined the circle of eight or so people, feeling entitled, because I knew one of its members, Don, who was probably stoking himself up to do a round with Smaug the Dragon on Dave's behalf.

As my brain cleared a little, I saw that the circle was strangely constituted. There was Don, there were a couple of other guys I knew from security and the stage crew, there was what looked to be a techie and a roadie or two. But there were also two very unusual characters at the powwow. One was a kid who looked to be about fifteen. He had an ornate haircut, a pencil-drawn bookie's mustache, and a look of terror on his face. He was jittering and shaking and quaking, trying to make it look like a dance of some kind and doing a pretty good job of it. Beside him was a middle-aged woman who I decided was his mother. She was short and a little hefty and completely at ease: she bore herself like a duchess.

Rock small talk went back and forth: the size of the crowd, the heft of the amps, the quality of the inebriates in this venue or that. I was now awake and feeling impatient. The crowd was feeling impatient, too. There were chants and rumblings. The show, I now gathered, was supposed to have started a while ago.

"So who's the band, anyway?" I asked.

Suburban mom looked at me in a none too genial way. Her eyes, I noticed, seemed to be purple, and a strange light was coming from them. "We are," she said. Her son, the kid who, as I saw it, was skipping school and feeling guilty because now he was getting a D in geometry, nodded his head with great approval.

"Who are *we*?" I wanted to know.

"Would you," one of the band's roadies said, "be willing to do a favor?"

"What?" It turned out that there was a problem with the placement of one of the amps; it turned out that this amp was at the peak of a very high pile. Adjustment was needed.

"It's not really that high," he said, and he pointed in the general direction of the clouds. The duchess looked at me as though the amp adjustment might be a real favor to her, too.

"You're not afraid of heights?" someone asked me.

"No, not really." Untrue. A vicious lie. When I look down from the top of a dozen or so stairs, I feel as if I'm staring at the world from the crest of Montezuma's pyramid. I do not like it. The psychoanalysts say that those of us who fear heights do so because when we're up high, we have to struggle hard against a potent urge—it's the death drive operating— to toss ourselves off and end it. I believe that I do not like heights because I'm congenitally clumsy and could easily slip and slide—much against my will—and be swallowed by the void. But then, the shrinks probably tell you, that's what they all say.

Why didn't I tell the roadie to go fix the amp himself? It was probably more his business than mine. But I was muzzy from sleep, still a little disoriented, and the beer and the sacrament weren't helping. I went over to the amp stack. No mountain climber has ever studied a sheer rock face the way I studied that configuration of amplifiers. I plotted one mode of ascent, then another; I trashed my plans and began again. Finally I figured it out, or I thought I did. I shoved a foot into an interamp crevice, and I began my ascent. It was not really very high, my goal. It was not really very dangerous, the climb. But for me it was high and dangerous. As I made my shaky ascent, I saw the duchess begin to move toward the stage, along with her kid; with them came four or five guys, a couple carrying guitars; the kid had one of the fanciest I'd seen. It seemed to have two necks, maybe it had three. After he was finished playing it, he could probably ride it home.

I made my way to the top of the amp pile and looked out at the 3 million, give or take, in front of me, lolling impatiently in the grass, like the crowd waiting to hear the Sermon on the Mount and then be off on their way. The band began futzing with their instruments, tuning up and strolling around. Suburban duchess turned her back to the crowd, and looked up in my direction. "Well?" she said silently, or maybe she didn't; maybe she was simply staring at the sky. After some pretty dangerous no-hands-holding-on-to-anything action— dangerous at least if you have my powers of balance—I had performed the amp adjustment. I stared out at the crowd and waited.

The drum banged once and again, and the kid with his bookie's mustache and too-styled hair leaned back and, barely touching his guitar, made it cry out with the sound that, no doubt, angels make when they experience ecstasy— not religious revelation but tearing, painful, screaming sex bliss—for the first time. It's probably with a mortal and it's probably something that they shouldn't do, but they do it and they like it and they sound off. Duchess of the well-mannered lawns and the impeccably paved driveways turned and faced the crowd and let go a banshee wail. She wasn't suburb mom now; she was Witch of the Storm and had a voice that circled through the trees and up and out of the clouds. It was purple, this voice, and red and orange and yellow, too. (I heard it and *saw* it: I know.) And the crowd rose up onto its feet all at once, like an enormous flower coming instantly into bloom, a many-toned, many-celled flower, strangely composed, weirdly made, yet organic and whole in itself.

The flower swayed gorgeously under the bright sun and under the Witch's song, which turned in time into a song about standing together and about overwhelming anything that made the standing impossible. "Tear down the walls," she wailed, but then sadly, desperately, meekly—for it was no longer 1968, and the things that were supposed to have happened in the way of peace and solidarity and love had not all come to pass—she whispered to me and the 3 million (give or take): "Won't you try?"

And I thought that maybe I would like to—in part maybe because I had the best seat in the house for all this and saw her work her womanly Prospero-like magic on that crowd and believed somehow that it was good, wicked and lovely and loving at once, as all good things of a sort probably should be.

I saw Dave down below on the corner of the stage. He was bedecked in his red satin sports jacket, his top-tier bit of rock finery, and wearing a Rolling Stones baseball hat, a numbered, limited-edition cap, no doubt. He gave me a grade-seven exasperation look. *Come down! Now!* I affected not to understand. Then he actually made a physical move—something Dave did not like to do. He generally controlled a scene with facial expressions exclusively; he seemed to feel significantly diminished when he had to speak. He beckoned me with his arm to get off the amp stack. But I looked away. I pretended not to see him. This moment was what I'd come to rock for and had waited for so many months to find. I'd stacked a thousand amps for it and eaten inedible food and listened to inane coke raps and consorted with crackbrained Hells Angels. Now the Witch was doing her thing—setting something like my Central Park acid vision to music—and I was going to take it in. A human being could capture that violent, tender feeling of being at one with all, could render it in words and sounds, and could make the crowd rise up like a force of loopy, loving seraphim. I stayed up there on my amp; I wasn't really interested in what Dave had to say at all.

After the show was over, Dave called the stage crew together and informed us that because it was a free concert, none of us would be getting paid. He seemed to look at me with particular delight as he said this. As to the Jefferson Starship (recently the Jefferson Airplane), for that of course is who was onstage that day, with Grace Slick playing the part of Magnolia Drive Duchess and Storm Witch, they seemed to have had a fine time that afternoon. The band came off and hugged the techies and the roadies and the stagehands—hugged me. And make of that rock-and-roll moment what you will, the song that eventually moved me so, "Volunteers," is about the only big song from the period that hasn't been gutted by being played on top of ads for Jeep Wranglers or online trading companies, or even getting any airtime to speak of on the radio, during the Golden Oldies Hour. The words "Up against the wall, motherfuckers" still aren't negotiable in the omnipresent all-day, all-night mall of America. Though not to be left entirely behind, the Starship in time began cutting pop anthems like

"We Built This City on Rock and Roll," a song that the Monkees could have covered with cool to spare.

Still, it woke me up—that moment—that blooming flower of humanity, the garden rising and appearing under the Witch's spell: rock had one more jolt for me when I thought it was gone and done for. This time the force and promise were of a political sort, I suppose—the music filled me with the promise of collective being, collective solidarity, collective change. It wasn't so much about nature, as my other moment in the park had been; it was about the people who, as the saying went, once united will not be defeated, who having once been nothing will in time be all. It was about Utopian promise, Utopian hope. But what to do in my own life, isolated and rather small, about all that force and beauty—alas, again I had little idea.

And there was something else, too. As much as I loved those moments on the amps and on the hill, I still had my doubts about them. Who is there, I wondered, who wants to be a part of a human whole—or a natural one—all of the time? ("And though one says that one is part of everything," says Stevens, ". . . it is an exertion that declines.") Pelops, the champion of the people, who loved the masses after his fashion, spent days alone in his room reading about them. When it came time to immerse himself in the crowd, he wasn't always game. Stuck downtown, about to descend into the teeming subway, I could often depend on Pelops to say, "Homer, it is too much for me. We must bourge-out. We must take a cab." (*Bourge-out* was a Pelops coinage, used to describe eating in restaurants, taking cabs, hiring cleaning people, and all the rest.) I loved such moments: I could criticize Pelops for retrograde tendencies *and* get myself a cab ride uptown. Pelops, always generous, always paid.

• •

On a chilly bright morning weeks after the Starship show (and a few other shows best forgotten), having deposited an outrageous number of months' rent with Pelops and cleaned my room and shoved most of my belongings into a duffel bag, I rose early and traipsed down to Broadway. It took a long time to get a cab—there were almost never any up at 187th Street—but finally one came. I tossed my duffel in like a body bag, and as we cruised off to the airport, I watched the sun edging over the top of the ugly tan sack. I felt way down in the mouth. I thought about Pelops and felt that however impossible he could be, he was better than anyone I knew at fending off the dull times. I spared some wistful thoughts for Dave, who now took on the guise of a man capable and settled and wise beyond his years.

But mainly I thought about my own situation. I was leaving New York as a failure. The way I saw it that day, New York was something like a sports franchise, and every year it summoned a horde of young people, rookies, to town. There were official draft choices who came with jobs at banks and art galleries, and there were the undrafted free-agent types like me. Then New York did its trick of shaking out and sieving through, separating goats and sheep, and in the end, after a year or two, most of the weak had come to understand themselves in their weakness. They hit the road. They were cast out of the grimy, corrupt metropolis, which was nonetheless the place on earth where things went on at three times the common intensity. It was like living in a movie—living in this place where life was more than life. At least it was like living in a movie until the director, which was the Darwinian spirit that did the choosing, let you know it was time to go, put you on waivers, or simply fired your ass.

I found the whole thing an enormous humiliation, especially given the chances that I'd had. I'd been given plenty of data. I'd had the best possible instruction: Pelops and Duggan and Duggan Senior and Grace Slick and King Crimson, not to mention a blast of lysergic acid diethylamide and my regal tree. The local Kings of Rock and Roll hadn't neglected me. They had striven on my behalf. They'd taught me all they could. Yet *it*, the great good thing, was still nowhere in sight. Whatever way you looked at it, my ass was fired. I couldn't cut it. I had to go.

"This isn't about a lot of John Denver crap," the Outward Bound boss told us as we sat around a campfire on our first night. "This isn't 'Rocky Mountain High, Colorado,' nonsense. This is something entirely different." The man was a liar, or at least half one, but we did not know as much, so we took it in and nodded with woodsmanlike gravity. There were a couple dozen of us, guys in our twenties and one young woman, who appeared to be about sixteen but was probably a little older. Her name was Christie, and she was of an oddly mixed appearance. She had the hard look of someone who's done a couple of years in the young women's reformatory, but also, seen from another angle, illuminated differently by the firelight, she had the inanely obedient look of someone who's been bludgeoned into sweetness by too many sermons, perhaps of the Mormon variety. The only other woman on our three-week expedition-to-be was the one who was going to head my group of twelve guys. She was small, about five feet, with amply muscled legs, which changed shape in half a dozen ways when she took a step, and a plain, intelligent face. She seemed somehow both confident and mildly confused.

She told us that her name was Carol and that she was a medical student.

She also retold us what the boss-hiker, who was pretty clearly her boyfriend, had said. This trip wasn't about John Denver and sweetness and light and lovely nature. It was about something altogether different.

By day, there was nothing sentimental about Outward Bound. By day, what we had was preparation for going Airborne, then after that, joining the Rangers. We pounded our way uphill and down; we slid through fields of broken rock and clambered up them again; we learned the rudiments of mountain climbing, and when we learned those, we climbed. We climbed a lot. The climbing tore all the skin from my knees and ripped my hands apart.

After a few days of this, I was able to add one more thing to the now apparently interminable list of what the gods had not designed me to do. It seemed that I had even less knack for climbing mountains than I did for playing inside linebacker or writing novels. I was strong enough. All that time hoisting amps had its payoff. But it was mostly upper-body strength. Climbing is about using your legs, and mine had to propel not just a torso swollen from my stagehand bodybuilding program, but also a gut mildly enlarged from dispatching too many beers and too many shots of tequila. On top of this difficulty, there was the fact that late-summer weather in the Colorado mountains has all the constancy of a high-end courtesan. It's sunny for a while, and that's grand, but then a storm comes whipping in and jumps on your back like a slave driver. The wind gets annoyed and, schoolyard bully–like, tries to shove you off the side of the mountain, way down, down.

It was awful. I pretended that I was climbing the cliffs on

D-day to blow up the German gun emplacement and end the barrage. I pretended that I was climbing up the mountain to the witch's castle to set Dorothy free. But these regressions did me no good. During the day, I hated the outdoors; I hated Colorado; I hated the Outward Bound School. At night, I may have hated them more, for at night we did two things: we sat around the fire performing amateur surgery on our blisters, and we listened to Carol go on in her madly bland way about the beauties of nature—its grandeur, its sublimity, its wonder. Rocky Mountain High, Colorado. She spoke—and in time some of us also spoke—about nature's power to cleanse away the accumulated corruption that civilization brings. Nature's purifying powers got plenty of attention. Its ability to dispense grace and save the souls of its communicants was a big theme. Left to ourselves out in the wild, we might become gentler, wiser, one with the rhythms of the earth. Nature could make us whole.

The next day, it was back to Green Beret training. It was surprising that they never showed us how to plant explosives or how to assassinate the wayward headman of a village. Then, at night, another installment in the continuing saga of how nature never betrays the heart that loves her.

This drove me nuts. I longed for Pelops and critique and sidewalks and alienation. When Carol got on a major roll, I would sometimes flash to what had now become one of my favorite New York images. It was of a black man with a well-trimmed beard, wearing an expensive leather coat, walking up Broadway with pirate-length strides, swigging from a bottle of Colt 45. He did not seem drunk or poor or drug addled. In fact, he seemed in a fine mood. About twenty-five yards in front of me, he pulled the last swig from the bottle, took the neck in his hand, raised the vessel overhead, and smashed it down on the sidewalk in a glowing exclamation of glass. As he passed me, he laughed and cried out, "The motherfucker! The motherfucker!"

Some of the other trekkers, too, were not responding well to Carol's combination of nature worship and boot-camp command. They were beginning to speculate about her sex life. They were beginning to refer to her as Mom.

Time labored on. We did something called the solo, on which you spend three days alone in the woods without food. I read the volume of Proust that I'd smuggled off onto the three-day, delighting in his ultracivilized ways. I also tried catching a trout with my hands. I was sure that this was not so hard to do; I'd seen Robert Redford accomplish it in a movie, *Jeremiah Johnson.* You merely had to stand in the stream with your hands close together and wait for a fish to swim in between. There were plenty of trout in the water, and in time one would have slid its way into my trap. But the water was cold. I couldn't keep my hands in trout-capture position for more than ten seconds. And then, if I did catch one, where was I supposed to cook it? Was I really going to rub sticks together?

"For a long time I used to go to bed early." That's the famous first line of Proust's seven-volume masterpiece. I read it over and over again, and I took it literally. I went to bed early and often. During the solo, I snoozed every chance I could. I ate nothing and drank stream water, and I slept like a yellow dog during high summer in Georgia. When I woke up, I knocked down another paragraph or two of Proust, took a walk, and went back to snoozing again.

At the end of the solo, we had a week or so left, and all

anyone could think of was getting to the last day of the trek. We were going to get a real meal. No more dry Green Beret rations. And we were going to do something else, too. This thing was pure and natural and even Native American: we were going to have a sweat lodge. Anticipation of the end grew. There was much talk about what delicacies we'd consume first when we finally came off the trail. There were wistful paeans to television and stereo sets and steak and corn. Emily Post never praised civilization as much as we did in the days leading up to the finish. Carol—Mom—did not get so much praise. She was beginning to grate on us all. We were tired of being driven like sled dogs during the day and then listening to her variations on John Denver at night. Were we also twelve guys sick of being told what to do by a woman?— one who was strikingly capable and smart, but without the least tang of salt or twist of jazz about her. I suppose so.

Carol, I suspect, thought of herself as a "good person": she was dutiful, she was a fine leader, and she was going to be a doctor. And yet there were the forced marches uphill and down, the blisters and the scrapes we sustained, and in these things she seemed to take no little pleasure. She'd smile at our complaints and push us harder. If you'd suggested to Carol that she had a bit of a mean streak, she'd have been so incensed that she'd have tried to send you home.

None of this justifies what happened on the last night. That night, we finally joined the other troop of hikers, the one that had gone off with Carol's fiancé, the one with Christie, who by all accounts had had a rough time with the commando-training aspect of the trek. The two dozen of us went to work and built a sweat lodge. We used rubber ground cloths and stones and got a fire going inside. It was an amazing success—in an hour or two, it was hot as the devil's kitchen in the lodge, and groups of us were going in, sitting, Indian-style of course, and then, after not too long, making our way out. We did this entirely unclothed. Carol included.

One can only imagine what a relief it must have been to Carol, getting to the end of the three weeks with a pack of semiferal guys, who talked mostly about rock bands and television and politics and sports and drugs. Finally she could exhale. Finally she could pull the pins out of her hair. She stayed in the sweat lodge about three times longer than any of us, and when she emerged, unclothed, she was lobster red and had a loopy grin on her face. She looked like she was coming out of a bar—maybe a bar in heaven, where clothing is optional. She looked very loose and happy and way more welcoming than she'd ever been on the trip.

She half collapsed, half sat down on a folded tarp not far outside the sweat lodge, and she was grinning. I passed her on the way into the pleasant inferno. I checked out her very muscular, appealing body (guys are compelled to do this) and ducked inside. With me was Christie: she turned out to be a reader, probably the only other one on the trip, and we were talking about Jack Kerouac and Allen Ginsberg and Ken Kesey's *Sometimes a Great Notion*, which we both loved. When Christie and I stepped out five or so minutes later—I have an Irishman's aversion to intense heat—Carol was lying down, still unclothed, her eyes partially closed, smiling. She was surrounded by five or six of the guys from my group. One of them had a pinecone in his hand. Hold it—almost all of them were cradling pinecones. As I walked closer, I saw one—a hefty blond guy—lightly toss his cone at Carol's semisleeping form. Then came another pinecone, then another. Then came a bunch. The expressions on the guys' faces were not friendly; they were not benign. This was not "Rocky Mountain High, Colorado." Carol kept smiling, with her eyes half open. The pinecones began to rain harder.

I don't know what I would have done if I'd wandered over to this scene on my own: I like to think it would have been the right thing, the good thing. But it might have been tempting to go along with Carol's smile for a while and to pretend that I didn't really know what was up. The scene had an ugly vibe. It had a pre-gang-rape, pre-assault vibe, even though it was about something as trivial as tossing a few pinecones. I felt this, anyway, and Christie, who was coming out of the sweat lodge at the same time, surely did, too.

Though apparently Christie had almost flunked commando training and had almost been sent home for her ineptitude (which probably wasn't much worse than mine), she seemed to know something that Carol, the trainer, did not. When she and I walked into the sweat lodge together, she was wearing cutoff shorts and a T-shirt. "Do you think I'm going to take my clothes off in front of you guys after you've been in the woods for three weeks? You must be crazy," she said. She sat getting basted inside her clothes. When we came out and saw the pinecone assault—which still ranks among the weirder moments of my life—we said, "Cut it out!" She may have said it first, but I hope that I managed to say it at about the same time. It was quiet for a moment. The guys looked at us like we were missing the point. But Christie held their stare. Then they stopped. There were lots of remarks about just playing and just fucking around and that was all it was and anyone who thought otherwise was fucked up, and all the rest. But then it grew quiet, and the guys got the sheep look on that can come when the wolf's been unexpectedly exposed. We all stood in a ring, staring down softly at our leader. In not too long, Carol was asleep. One of the guys who had been tossing cones down on her covered her up gently with a down-filled bag. I'm surprised he didn't bend over and kiss her on the forehead. She looked peaceful and childishly innocent.

Of course, that's probably what our whole trek had been about from Carol's point of view—peace and childlike innocence. That's what she wanted to find in nature. But who, at least from time to time, doesn't? The intense vulnerability and charm of natural things that I'd felt that day on my hill in Central Park was in line with Carol's mode of seeing things. (The ferocity of nature that I'd also experienced then wasn't part of this way of looking at matters at all.) The faith in pure nature rose up in all its beauty during the sixties, and I, like almost everyone else who was young then, felt it beckoning.

But as lovely as worship of a kind nature can be, I saw that night that it's a dangerous thing, too. It puts you off your guard. It lets the snake slip too smoothly into the garden. No one coasting on a Rocky Mountain High would be able to see the serpent for what he was—he'd just be that shining insinuating form that Eve delights in ("Pleasing was his shape / And lovely")—until he's done his business.

On my trek into Colorado, I'd encountered a vision of nature as a repository of humane and humanizing virtues and, somewhat unknown to myself, that's probably what I'd gone into the mountains to find. I'd wanted to purify myself of the shit and slime and sludge that were New York. Yet though I'd seen some unpleasant things in the city—to walk outside was to see unpleasant things—I'd not seen anything quite as disturbing as that weird pinecone episode. The incident wasn't purely toxic—in a way, the guys *were* just playing. It was the fact that it had a toxic core that no one was acknowledging, which could have broken out full-strength, that made the scene unnerving. What also struck me that night, based on the looks on the faces of the guys who formed the circle, guys who had seemed to me reasonably good-hearted, was simple enough, known to almost all women, but still disturbing. Women may resent men, and that resentment can bear many different sorts of poison fruit. They may undermine them, browbeat them, neuter them emotionally. It happens all the time. But men—and I would dare say almost all men—are capable of genuinely hating women: of ruining them, raping them, killing them. It isn't part of the pure-nature ideology, this hatred, but that night made me sure that it was out there nonetheless.

Nature wasn't *it* for me, at least not nature as sanitized by Carol and John Denver. But then, Grace's keening voice, with all its anger and ferocity as well as its intense beauty and hope, could probably have told me as much and saved me a plane ride out, a few weeks of basic training, and a very, very long hitchhike back to the East.

6

DISCO NIGHTS

(eros)

Pennsylvania, I decided as I bumped along in the passenger's seat of an enormous tractor-trailer truck, was a state in need of serious editing. It went on way, way too long. The truck driver and I were trying to stay awake across its expanse by counting the deer that had come to graze on the median strip and on the grassy shoulder of the turnpike. Halfway across the state, we'd counted over a hundred: a lot of Pennsylvania, a lot of deer. I'd begun hitchhiking in Denver after my graduation without honors from the Colorado Outward Bound School, and I'd been hitching now for four days. I desperately wanted to get to the end of that interminable state, Pennsylvania, but then, too, I desperately did not. At the end, as we approached Jersey, I was going to have to make a choice. I needed to decide whether to hop off, go back to New York, and throw myself on the mercy of Pelops and Dave or stay with the driver and head to Massachusetts, where I'd grown up.

I thought about New York, and what mostly came to mind were its miseries. I was always running out of money. I was tired of eating liver in its myriad forms. By the time I left, I was even a little sick of Pelops Kazanjian and his raps about the workers and the peasants and the impending overthrow of the international bourgeoisie—they were sounding more and more like intellectual air guitar. And I was tired of Dave, who at the stadium was perpetually staring at me with dead-eyed frustration. Dave had held me in vague awe while I sat upstairs for hours trying to write my stream-of-consciousness antinovel, making the noise of an all-night firing squad, but when the machine died and my writing aspirations withered, he had a hard time figuring out what the point of me was. Duggan had gone off to Oxford to study literature—the last piece of advice his favorite Bennington teacher gave him was not to bend over when he was alone with his tutor—and so the one certifiably sane person of my age I knew in Manhattan wouldn't be around.

When it was time to decide—the moment when you make your leap of faith or you don't—I didn't. I hadn't enough faith in myself to venture a few more rounds with New York after the drubbing it had given me already. I stayed in the rig, deer-counting (we demolished all previous records), and clambered off at an exit not far from the city of Northampton, Massachusetts. Despite my Colorado rock-climbing experience, I still managed to stumble and almost sprain an ankle getting out of the truck.

Northampton is in the western part of the state, where the so-called five colleges are to be found: Amherst, the University of Massachusetts, Smith, Hampshire, and Mount Holyoke. In the midseventies the area was hard-core sixties. (It still is.)

If the region had had a flag—and given its residents' sense of themselves, it should have—the flag would have been cut diagonally, with a marijuana leaf rampant in one sector and the peace sign psychedelic in the other. I knew the place well. I'd gone to college for a year and a half at U Mass before making my move to Bennington, which was like going from an all-out raucous party to a raucous party interspersed with cunning party-commentary and interpretation. (Also, people would temporarily check out of the Bennington party to go skiing in Switzerland; they'd check out of the U Mass party to go work in a factory to come up with the next term's tuition, which was three hundred bucks.) I had friends around Northampton, a few of them wise enough to string out their college lives to eight years or so. I showed up in town unannounced, met my old pals (we called each other bro-dogs), exchanged many soul-style handshakes, sat in circles passing the signifier, and slept on a variety of living-room floors.

Eventually I rented a room in a three-decker mongrel of a house with a couple of roommates, both women, one a waitress, the other a mover in western Massachusetts's burgeoning social service world, and began doing what I then did surpassingly well (and still am no slouch at), which is to say, not very much at all. The rent was about a $120 a month, a sum I drew from my small pile of rock-and-roll savings. I went back to eating beef liver (calves' on special occasions) and to spending the day in the public library, reading all things that fell into my hands and dreaming of what I someday might write. Yet I knew writing to be work. I had tried it in New York and confirmed as much. On the matter of actually writing, I was somewhat the way Saint Augustine once was on chastity: "Lord," he said, "make me chaste, but not yet." "Lord

Apollo," I thought then, "make me a writer, but please, not yet."

Apollo was happy to comply. I did somehow score a used electric typewriter and got into machine-gunner mode from time to time, after I'd had my mandatory six cups of coffee and chewed contemplatively on the grounds, but the results were pretty much what they'd been in New York. Fortunately, I didn't show the stuff around. When Molière's Misanthrope judges a friend's work to be third-rate, the miffed friend asks if *he* could do better. "I might, by chance" the Misanthrope declares, "write something just as shoddy; / But then I wouldn't show it to everybody." That about summarized my position.

Nor did I need to pray to Lord Yahweh or anyone else to maintain my chastity. It was doing absolutely fine on its own. A librarian from the public library followed me home once or twice, but she wasn't my type. As she looked across my room at the dissolute pile of books, a few from *her* library, I could feel her body lightly vibrating with the wish to get at them, stack them, order them, and code the strays into the Dewey Decimal System. Had I meandered off to the bathroom for a piss and left her alone with the mess, I'm sure she would not have been able to contain herself. Then she would have hit my correspondence, dating and filing the letters that Duggan had been sending me from Oxford, where he was working with the renowned Terry Eagleton. My librarian went home frustrated. As for me, I dreamed and noodled and read promiscuously and kept in pretty good physical shape, running through the gray streets of Northampton, occasionally chugging past the church where Jonathan Edwards—he of "Sinners in the Hands of an Angry God" fame—delivered his sermons. I also swam in the pool at the local YMCA, which was not at all hard to sneak into without a membership. Mostly I went my indolent Wildean way—Wilde without the quips and the quiddities and all the brilliant jottings, just the Irish laziness.

One day I picked up a local newspaper, and my eye fell on an ad. Someone was opening a discotheque, no doubt modeled on New York's notorious Studio 54, and needed bartenders. My bartending experience consisted largely of opening bottles of beer—Heineken if possible, Budweiser more likely—and then drinking them. My bag of rock-and-roll gold was growing light, and I was getting a little worried about my ceaseless reading. I feared that I was spending too much time letting other people think all my thoughts for me. I was afraid that I was reading myself stupid. Besides, who couldn't tend a bar in Northampton? It would be easy, lucrative work.

A slight, bespectacled guy with a tie on—where were they coming from, I wondered, men my age who wore ties?—hired me, not as a bartender but as the doorman. "How good are you with your hands?" he asked. "I mean, really. If somebody causes trouble, you could handle them, right?" I realized that if I assented and got the job and grabbed myself a salary, however meager, I could stop with the liver and maybe go buy a hamburger or two at a place called Fitzwillie's, the first fern bar I'd seen, which featured many gorgeous waitresses, one of whom especially appealed to me because it was rumored she'd been a history major at Princeton, another of whom because, though she already looked as slinky as she could look in her Fitzwillie's leotard, she'd changed her name from Catherine to Primala, or something like that, and the combination of the Puritan moniker with the slink and the slither caught my attention, and another of whom because . . . , but enough. I gave Max to understand that I was a formidable guy with my dukes, and he hired me on the spot.

On Grand Opening Night at Phase II, I was standing at the door in jeans, boots, a white shirt, and a vest snagged from the local Goodwill store. I was checking IDs. But as the meager crowd scraped in, I was also copping an Oxford University education, free.

Duggan kept me informed about Oxford in letters of prodigious length, typed on yellow paper so thin that the keys were constantly blowing holes in it, making the sheets look like fields where land mines had recently gone off. In the first letter, he'd given me three salient facts about Oxford and his college, Mansfield. He said that it was always freezing, that there was never enough to eat (he claimed they cut the roast beef so thin that you could see through it to the other side), and that after it rained, the streets of Oxford filled up with used condoms. The English apparently found drizzle an aphrodisiac. Duggan had also been assigned a figure called a scout, who was supposed to see to his personal needs. The scout came into Duggan's room every day, took his enormous steamer trunk, hoisted it on top of Duggan's convict-size bed, which was already amok with books and papers and scarves and gloves and other pieces of Dugganania, and then left. The upper-class Brits at Oxford had some strange locutions: When one was going to take a piss, he announced that he was off to "point Percy at the porcelain." A bowel movement was—disgustingly enough—"choking a Darkie."

Besides information on the scout, the idiom, the condoms, and his tutor, an Anglo-Saxon scholar apparently allergic to bathwater, Duggan kept me abreast on what he was reading. What Duggan read, I read; in fact, often what he read, I memorized.

The first night at Phase II, I had in my pocket, and partway in my mind, Robert Browning's poem "My Last Duchess." As I looked over drivers' licenses and birth certificates and tried to do the birthday math, I intoned to myself the words,

> *That's my last Duchess painted on the wall*
> *Looking as if she were alive. I call*
> *That piece a wonder, now: Frà Pandolf's hands*
> *Worked busily a day, and there she stands.*

I savored the duke's feline nastiness—he's had his last duchess killed for failing quite to please him, and now he's negotiating for another wife—and also savored Browning's insinuating rhymes. The poem actually end-rhymes all the way through—wall/call, hands/stands—but the ear barely knows it, the conscious ear anyway. "Heard melodies are sweet, but those unheard / Are sweeter," Keats says. This was something like an unheard melody. Such stuff filled me with lazy pleasure, often the best kind.

Pelops would probably have approved this reading and memorizing at the door; he would have seen it as an index of my alienation, though he would have wished I'd been consulting more revolutionary texts. He was proud of the fact that he'd been tossed off the rock crew for reading the commie classics. But during those days, I heard little from Pelops. To him, New York was absolutely all there was. When you left the city, you fell off the edge of the known world, and that was the end of you. Pelops hung around in my thoughts, though, no doubt about that. He represented left-wing righteousness, and I often plopped him in the judgment seat and let him pass sentence on my current doings. Could anyone have picked a more decadent King Conscience? And Pelops did not go easy on me. He told me that overall, here at Phase II, I was wasting my life. I was betraying my class origins. When was I going to get off my ass and do something for the people?

Inside Phase II, the disco world was coming into full swing. There were lords in sharp shirts, with collars flaring out like vestigial wings, medallions glowing on their exposed chests, and pompadours, sprayed helmetlike, the kind of style that no doubt provoked Warren Zevon to his most memorable line—albeit about a werewolf: "His hair was perfect." The ladies wore heels and minidresses and push-up bras and—I'd learn—naughty lingerie of all sorts. Donna Summer and KC and the Sunshine Band provided machined waves of easily metabolized tunes for the gentry, who were occasionally enjoined to halt and, together as one, do the Bus Stop or perform the Hustle, corporately created dances for the new Saturday-night aristocrats.

The disco rebellion was an aristocratic revolution from below, from below the college kids who had strained so hard to deny their privileges and to merge in a classless multitude. Now the kids that the college crowd had left behind in Brooklyn and the Bronx and Medford and Somerville were having their day, and what they wanted was "class." They wanted to dress with class; they wanted to act classy; one of their standard insults was to let someone know that he "had no class." Which is just what the folks at Woodstock wanted, wasn't it?—to have no class at all.

The disco kids worked all day at beauty salons and auto-parts stores; they drove delivery trucks and typed letters in grim office buildings, and they lived at home, with their parents. When they got their checks on Friday, they wanted to spend them, the faster the better. Some of the college kids followed them onto the disco floor and donned the Louis XIV duds, but the Vietnam War was over, the draft was past and gone, and many of them were disappearing into the hipper precincts of middle-class life. The people I'd gone to Bennington with were now well installed in the History of Consciousness program at U Cal–Santa Cruz (Hist-Con it was called); or they were in their second year at law school, talking about doing a lot of pro bono stuff and sticking it to the rogue corporations (but their loans were swelling up and up); or they'd become editorial assistants, then assistant editors at Knopf. And here was I, swaying gently (and, being me, out of time with the music) at the door of Phase II to the sounds of "Love to Love You Baby"—like being washed over by a warm pink ocean—memorizing Browning and living in a spectacularly ugly house on the near side of nowhere.

But my slot in life was fascinating. The sixties, assuming they had ever existed in the first place, were being terminated, and I was there for the next phase, Phase II. Just as the French Revolution had changed the calendar, the restored aristocrats sought quickly to switch it back. I was living in the midst of a grand antirebellion, antirebellion from below. Yet I couldn't figure out for anything why this was taking place. The world of Woodstock had its contradictions and absurdities, sure, but the disco world, as I looked out on it, seemed absolutely inane. Why would anyone want to dress this way? Why would anybody buy a record by KC and the Sunshine

Band and then spend Saturday afternoon at home in front of the mirror, learning the ridiculous dances that went with it?

There was one consolation, albeit a pretty shallow one. In this antirebellion, or at least its Northampton, Massachusetts, installment, I was not an inestimable figure. Not long after I got the job at Phase II, my friend Fred, a guy not easily impressed, had a dream that featured me center stage. I was in the midst of the disco floor, with lights throbbing all around me. So as to make the lights shift and pulse harder, I was stomping on the floor. A crowd gathered around me. They liked what they saw. "Man," one said, "that guy has some strong thighs." "Strong thighs!" the crowd took up the chant. "Strong thighs!" I was the security man as hero. I was the guy who both stoked and disciplined the new Dionysian force abroad in the world. When Fred told me his dream, I flashed on an image from a Grateful Dead show where the crowd had gone berserk: a mountainous Hells Angel stood on the edge of the stage, twenty feet above the foaming multitude trying to break down the fences and climb in. He unzipped his fly, took out his business, and pissed down for what seemed like five minutes on their bobbling heads; as he did so, he guzzled from a quart bottle of beer, as though to replenish the stream and keep it running. In silhouette, black against the twilight sky, he looked like an outdoor fountain in a pleasure garden that Lord Hades might have designed for himself.

The people who worked at Phase II all seemed about as lost as I was. I had put the quest for the great good thing, the quest for the elusive *it*, pretty much on hold. I was hunkering down, going into training, stocking my mind with prose and poems, stoking my body by running and weight lifting, and until I got to Phase II, preserving it with unvowed vows of chastity, too.

Many of the gang who worked at the Phase had gone to the University of Massachusetts, which had granted them degrees and pretty good educations, but had provided them with none of the connections that it often takes to get on in life, especially during hard economic times. Coming from Yale and Amherst, you have your classmates to rely on, and you often have the influence of their well-connected parents, too. One of the waitresses was a painter who didn't paint; another planned to use the job as a stepping-stone to great things, though what, she did not know (she wanted the doormen and bartenders to wear tuxedos); a third, Colleen, was truly generous, truly lost, charming and freckled and kind. The last time I saw her, about a year after the disco closed and we all went our ways, she was at a Halloween party, dressed in a too-big, pajama-floppy New York Yankees uniform. Her cap was pulled down over the right side of her face at an impossibly fetching angle. "How are you, Colleen?" I asked. "Not so great." It turned out that she had been caught smuggling heroin in from Mexico and was out on bail, waiting for the following Monday when she would begin a five-year stretch at the nearby women's reformatory.

I had some ambition then, however modest. At Phase II, I aspired not only to learn Browning but to acquire the arts of bartending. Bartending, it struck me, was not just a manly thing in itself, but a skill I could use to travel America and maybe the world. There's always a job for a good bartender, right? So one slow evening, I put myself under the tutelage of a tightly strung, bespectacled guy named Mel, a former business major, who was into bartending, he said, for the long haul.

He taught me a few rudiments: how to pour beer from the tap, getting the right head; how to mix some basic drinks— brandy Alexanders were popular at the time—and I cut loose on a few, consuming them after they'd been concocted so as not to be wasteful. Then Mel let me go to work for the small crowd milling around the Phase II bar. I had a merry time kibitzing with the line of communicants at my little altar rail, devotedly and with something of a priestly decorum adminis- tering the sacrament of booze. (The cash register, surrounded by neon beer signs, was my altar.) I delighted in the tips—no one tips the bouncer—and was highly pleased by my new rank and station.

At the end of the evening, Mel pulled me aside for a talk. He was frowning so hard I was afraid he was going to shatter the bridge of his glasses. He told me, in a tone generally em- ployed only by oncologists and heart specialists, that though I'd seemed game enough, I had—I recall the words exactly— "no real natural ability as a bartender." Huh? "I just didn't see it," he murmured. "The touch wasn't there."

I understood by then that there were many things for which nature had not made me. I was not cut out to be a physicist or an all-pro linebacker; my Hollywood acting career had no doubt ended on the day that I appeared in *Jaws*, slouched against a pylon, waiting for the Vineyard ferry to dock. But that it was possible to be unfit to be a puller of tap handles and a compounder of high-proof poisons—this was strange. Mel turned on his heel with a slightly mechanical effect and went off to inform the manager, the owner, and anyone else who would listen to him about my lack of natural aptitude for the higher arts of transferring liquid from one place to another. A few months later, Mel got into a loud dispute with a couple of raunchy-looking customers. He kept sending me rapid eyebrow-elevation signals, and I kept failing to comprehend them.

Being what was called the bouncer was part of my job, along with the checking of identifications and the clandestine memorization of Browning, and then—with a change in the program of Duggan's tutor—Alfred, Lord Tennyson. I became especially infatuated with Tennyson's "Ulysses"—bookish young men love to imagine that they're old and weary and have seen it all—and I recited the poem under my breath for at least a month. I did shiver a little, though, when I got to the part about serving and striving and not yielding, which was a part of the Outward Bound rhetoric and sent my thoughts back to my dismal days in nature.

Though I had no upper-level evaluator of standing to rely on and to give me an authoritative grade—no Melvin-like senior bounder—I believe that at this job I was superior. I had two rules, which I'd learned working at rock and roll: always talk very softly, and never touch anyone. When you raise your voice, you agitate people. When you put a hand on someone, however softly, you become part of the altercation.

One night a guy with a startlingly disfigured face stood up and began ripping across the room toward another table; he was rammed with what was plainly murderous intent. I'd noticed this guy at the door, and his face was a marvel. All of his features were twisted toward the right and seemed to be made of melting clay; it looked like a terrible cross between a birth trauma—a rogue doctor gone maniacal with the forceps—and horrible burns. I got between him and the laughing party of six and (softly) asked what was up. "They're taking pictures," he said. I saw no camera anywhere. I had no idea what he meant. But then, steeped as I was, thanks to Browning and Tennyson, in the language of metaphor, I figured out what he was talking about. He was being stared at and didn't like it. But to preserve his dignity, he needed an indirect way to express matters. In fact, he actually managed to flatter himself a little bit and to make of his disfigurement something of a gift. His persecutors were taking pictures: they were pathetic paparazzi, who made their living hounding stars.

I looked him clean in the eye—something that I suspected new acquaintances rarely did—and saw into what I took to be the depths of earth-ambulating purgatory. *You have no idea,* his expression told me. *Don't even think you can imagine it.* I tried to make my face say, *I know I can't, but it doesn't mean I can't help you out a little now.* "They're taking pictures," he said again. "They'll stop," I told him. I walked him over to his seat and gestured to sourpuss Melvin to send him a drink. Then, in dulcet tones, I talked to the paparazzi in the nearby booth about compassion for others, living and letting live, and what they might be drinking—for sending them a free round also seemed a good idea. Did I have to pay for these magnanimous gestures? They were tallied against an invisible and nonexistent thing called my tab.

It seems that the paparazzi were not completely content with the way I resolved the dispute. Apparently when they left, they went romping through the Phase II parking lot, tearing the aerials off the parked automobiles, swishing them through the air and making threats. One of the cars so denuded was my ten-year-old Ford. (I'd bought the car from a professor at Smith, who loved it so much that she wept lightly when she transferred it to me. It was, at the point of sale, the *cleanest* car in the world, both inside and out, a dispensation that did not last.) All of this was relayed to me by customers on the way in. Still, by the time I got out of the Phase, three in the morning or so, the malefactors were gone. I found the antenna, lying on the concrete like a dead wand, about twenty yards from the Ford.

I had about one semicrisis with customers per week and settled them all without a raised voice or a punch either way (though my tab must have grown out of all proportion). Eventually the place began to prosper, mildly, and a few other doormen-bouncers were hired. I was supposedly their boss. The challenge of the job doubled then, because some of them were reckless types who wanted to get into brawls, and they were on the lookout for customer transgressions of all sorts. I spent a fair amount of time getting between customers and colleagues. On the worst occasions the beef was between two colleagues.

Failed as a dispenser of drinks but a pretty potent, if lucky, success as a bouncer and doorman, I was happy enough each night to take up my position guarding the gate. I was Cerberus, the monster dog, at the door of paradise, or at least I was for the hordes of underage kids who were always aching to get in. They kept trying, and I kept denying them. When one of them would pass the bar of eighteen, the drinking age at the time, and actually be legit, it was time for a free drink on the mythic tab and general congratulations all around. They had joined the ranks of the disco generation with all the rights and privileges.

The job of standing around at the door fit me well. I love being in and out of the game at the same time. I love observing, brooding, but being able to run in off the bench and jump into the midst of the action. Maybe I found my métier at Phase II and should still be in the security biz, watching and waiting and leaping headlong when the occasion arises, and every now and then when it doesn't.

One of my favorite visitors at the Phase was Mike Murphy. Murph had come up to Northampton from Brooklyn to get away from the guns and drugs and weirdness. He loved what he thought of as his new rural tranquillity, and he sought peace wherever he could find it. Yet Murph was prone to agitation, and of this he was aware. I asked him once what sort of job he was doing—it was a given that all of us in Northampton had what we called shit jobs, assuming that we had jobs at all. Murph's shit job was sweeping out the half-dozen commercial buildings owned by a rich local hippie. Every morning, Murph got a note from the ponytailed magnate telling him what he was supposed to do. They only communicated by note, and Murph one day revealed to me that he actually hadn't seen his boss for about a year. How come? Because, Murph explained, if I actually face the guy and he tells me what to do and his voice gets the wrong tone in it, I can't guarantee what's going to happen. "You might smack him?" Murph indicated that he might. "I've got this slight problem with authority," he said.

When Murph came to the Phase, I tried to put him at a table he especially liked, slightly elevated, not far from the dance floor, where he could look down in bemusement at the goings-on. He sat there, hour on hour, nursing his white Russian (or his Caucasian, as the drink would in time be called) and philosophizing in his private key. Or at least he did until something agitated him. The thing that most agitated Murphy while he sat at Phase II, watching the Zeitgeist shift, was the arrival of his prime existential enemies, girls from Smith College, Smithies.

Why did Murph dislike Smith girls so much? A thousand deep reasons, I imagined, many class-based. Murphy was, like me, working-class Irish, and he was more determined than I was to stay put. But if you asked him about his problems with Smith girls, you were likely to hear a story, and a protracted one, about their wayward habits as pedestrians. It turned out that the girls drove Murph nuts because they crossed the street when and as they liked, moving diagonally, for instance, when they should have obeyed the light and gone block to block in a considerate foursquare way. I concluded that to Murphy, the girls' insouciance as pedestrians was a metaphor for how they did what they wanted, cut corners, and pretended that the world was there for them alone. I—the budding literary critic, who had done such fine work unpacking the "taking pictures" metaphor—broached this idea to Murphy. He looked at me with all the patience he could muster and told me that no, he simply hated jaywalking. End of story.

Years later, as a prof, I turned up in Northampton to give a lecture on the Gothic, based on a book I was at work on. I paraded down Main Street, passing troupes of wayward-walking Smith girls, and thought naturally of Murph. Soon there was Murphy himself, sitting outside a coffee shop and sipping his brew, though the weather was bitterly cold, and giving the street the same flaneur's eye that he'd deployed when he sat at his ease inside Phase II twenty years before. We recognized each other and sat and talked. He asked me the reason for my visit, and I told him that I was at Smith to give a lecture. He looked at me with great compassion. "You used to be something in this town," he said, "when you were

157   •

at Phase II. Now look at you. Entertaining Smith girls." I asked if their performance as pedestrians had improved any over the years. "Worse," he replied. "If anything, much worse."

Aside from my official gig as bouncer, I had another role at Phase II, mysterious and of brief duration, and that was as a guy rather attractive to women. How this happened I can't say. I was, as I had been and would be, neither especially homely nor handsome, far from rich, passably dressed, not infrequently bathed, but never powdered, much less scented; preoccupied, sterner in visage than I generally feel, and not altogether unhappy to be alive and on the scene. Somehow all of this rather unpromising mishmash proved magnetic. The wide-eyed, pony-strutting, hair-flouncing disco girls liked me, or some of them did. They invited me home, cooked me late-night breakfasts, shushed their sleeping children (a few had those), and made my life a thing of erotic variety and intrigue. (Once, a nurse—alright, a nurse-in-training— hollered across the disco floor the words, "I think Mark wants me to go home with him!")

To have such allure, I imagined that I would have to write three or four books, or a half-dozen—or at least produce one gritty blast of a novel, like Robert Stone's *Dog Soldiers*, which I read and reread in part so as to hide from the more obscure works of Browning and Tennyson and, more feared, the next figure on Duggan's reading list, Matthew Arnold. But truth be told, beauties don't usually care much for writers, who often have the habit of making them feel dumb. It's hard for a young man to believe that a beautiful woman can be anything but happy—she has her white magic working all the time, getting her attention, creating a seat at the bar, cutting the price on that skirt she has to have. (A friend once saw a lovely woman walking out of his shrink's offices, and all he could ask for his entire session was, "What's *she* doing here? How could *she* need therapy?" Eventually his fascination about this woman became a major focus of *his* treatment.) To get the girl's attention, the writer is witty—as he thinks he should be—and all too often that terrifies the beauty. Is she laughing at the right time? Should she laugh at all?

I once heard the lead singer of the Black Crowes say that he'd toyed with the idea of becoming a writer but that all the writers he knew had rotting teeth and never got anywhere with girls. In my disco guise, I was not the Writer and didn't try to be. (Someone might have asked to see my work.) No, if the women of the disco were Beauty—though often fabricated, cosmetic, low-couture Beauty—then I was, for a brief period, Strength, albeit scripted, premeditated, slightly anxious Strength. One of the reasons I was so adept as a bouncer was that I truly did not wish to get into brawls. Quiet strength (or the illusion thereof) seemed to sell, at least much better than mouthy intelligence. Norman Mailer described a gambit he used at dinner parties when things were getting dull. Each man looks at the woman beside him and says, "You're beautiful." She digests the compliment, then responds in the appropriate key. She looks her fella in the eyes and says, "You're brave." (No smirking allowed.) All spirits climb skyward.

As to the disco girls, well, beautiful as they may have been, they were not really my type, and I was not theirs. The era of free love—the ideology of omnipresent mutual human attraction—may have been over, but the era of runaway sex was not. This era, which will be looked back upon as the golden or the black age of Eros, depending on the viewer, took place in that small gap after the invention and dissemination of reliable birth control and before the advent of herpes, AIDS, and the other venereal comeuppances. The means were there, and people used them.

But of course Eros is a strong, strange god. The witty Greeks depicted him as a child, baby Cupid, rather than as the strapping giant he is. Sex activates a phenomenal complex of feelings, in women especially, but in men, too. In the small, often shabby apartments, with or without the cribs in adjoining rooms, I encountered a level of sadness and need, and often a fierce hope of being rescued, beneath the party girl's flounce and flourish. What began as transgressive fun often ended close to tears as the weight of the woman's thousand and one disappointments (of whom I was soon to be another) and the force of her still insistent if now maimed hope rose gradually to the surface. One lure of sex, for me, was the intimate conversation that could follow: talk that went beyond the everyday gibberish. (I've sometimes been envious of people who find themselves in Alcoholics Anonymous meetings because, as I understand it, there's a distinct shortage of bullshit there. The grief that makes up a considerable quotient of everyday life for most of us can get full articulation, and people actually tell something like the truth about how it feels to exist.) What I often heard from the disco girls was sad beyond expression. I heard about abortions endured alone—after foolproof birth control was fooled—and about horrible family lives: my nurse-in-training had a wicked stepmother who, I understood, enforced her will with a sawed-off broomstick.

There was no wild, deep attraction in any of these encounters, just human desire, jazzed by booze and the wild lights and the disco beat. There was also the wish not to be left out. Sex was everywhere. Sex was free. Don't be the last on your block. How could you not use a license that humanity had been aching to win for thousands of years—copulation divorced from pregnancy (most of the time).

None of the disco ladies felt a tidal pull to me, or I to them: it was not the divine madness of Eros. What happened at the disco, what happened all around the country at the time maybe, was simply lust crossed with license—and if the result was some bouncingly happy times, there were also moments so dismal that they almost eclipsed the others. For here, it began to occur to me, I was meeting something deep in the human condition: sorrow cuts deeper than joy. Our pains hurt longer and harder than our pleasures please. If you're looking for a formula for the creation of an animal prone to be awash in pain yet perpetually seeking the opposite, in part to make the pain recede, then there you have it.

There are sorrows, and indeed many of them, that can mar us in ways that almost no joy can restore. "A deep distress hath humanized my soul," says Wordsworth: that is, a loss—in this case the loss of his dear brother—made him a part of the community of suffering, from which there may be no return. Life is a thing of traumas. Are there antitraumas to be experienced? Maybe there are. The birth of one's first child can seem to salve many past sorrows. I didn't experience such deep, deciding sorrows in the disco-eros, but I did begin to imagine their shape as I touched a few brutally handled lives. (I still cannot forget that broomstick.) The life of the libertine—skipping from one bed to the next, like a rock skimming the surface of a lake, ever moving, never stopping—wasn't the life for me.

By the time you're an adult or close, most of your patterns are probably in place. Some people do have remarkably mobile erotic powers—they hook in fast and they disengage faster. (They're the ones who can concur with what my New York King, Woody Allen, said when he was informed that sex without love was an empty experience: "Yes, but as empty experiences go, it's one of the best.")

But most of us are far different. It takes us a while to settle on a lover, a while to trust, a while to submit. A sexual life full of shifts and twists only makes us dizzy. We step out of a hastily entered bed feeling like we've stepped off a twirling, whirling ride at the carnival. At the disco, I found that fast-moving Eros wasn't my game. It wasn't *it* for me. Through the pursuit of this so-called joy, my life became a more melancholy thing.

One weekend, a former girlfriend from Bennington came to visit. "I want," she said, "to check out your disco life." She was an anthropology major, and when she arrived, she went into something like anthropology mode. She began to investigate the tribe that was me. "I don't want to do anything special," she declared. "I want to do what you do in a day."

We spent the afternoon doing what I'd planned, questing for a cheap set of tires, maybe used tires even, for my Ford, the one with the missing aerial. But Renee was as merry as could be. We bounced tires back and forth at each other across a garage floor. She took a rabid interest in tread wear. She set out to master the theory of rotation. She spoke of warranties. She got down on her back and inspected the underside of my car, hoping to draw independent conclusions about this mystical thing called alignment.

Renee did not look at all disco. She wore blue jeans, stunningly utilitarian shoes, and a man's shirt—mine, I think. She was also wearing a pair of glasses with enormous frames embossed with rhinestones. When I asked her what was with the outfit and the glasses—I knew her to own a pair of contacts and to be able to turn most of the heads in a room if she wanted to—the antidisco spirit rose up in her, and she said, "When I wear them, men leave me alone." No shit.

After about three hours of being dragged through tire-world purgatory, she piped up and made a request. "One thing," she said. "There's just one thing that I want." On the way into town, driving a car for which I imagine her father acquired the tires and arranged the maintenance, she'd seen something holy, she said, and she wanted us to view it together. Renee had a weakness for Indian religions, and I imagined that I'd soon be forced into an audience with a saffron-dressed holy man who smelled of incense and mumbled sweetly, as if his mouth were full of dry cereal.

No, the something turned out to be a sign at a car dealership not far from the edge of town. It read: TIME FLIES LIKE THE WIND. / FRUIT FLIES LIKE BANANAS. For reasons that evade me still, I found this sign about as silly-deep-magnificent as Renee did. What happened to those words that day? If they'd occurred in a story, they might have been called a leitmotif; in classical music, a theme susceptible to no end of variations; in rock, a hook; in jazz, the basis for a near infinity of riffs. If you were in the backseat of my aerialless Ford, rolling along on my four unreplaced tires, each bald as the old moon, you might have called our interweaving of time and the wind, and bananas and fruit flies—which went on all day and into the night—boring, ridiculous, and beside the point. But in fact there was no one there to listen and to offer judgment: it was just the two of us.

SCHOOL DAYS

(depression)

All during my interview for a job teaching at a place called the Woodstock Country School, I was looking over the headmaster's shoulder and through a large picture window. There in the mucky space midway between the school administration building, where the headmaster and I were meeting, and its library, which had once been a stable, sat a young woman on a plastic chair. She was clutching a coffee cup, smoking a cigarette, and huddling in on herself like someone who has unaccountably survived destruction, massacre, or major dispossession and is not even beginning to deal with it all. Edward Hopper, dean of painterly depression, would have rejected her for being too morose, too far gone. The girl, I would later learn, was named Rose Ellen Brown, Rosie, and she was a very shy, talented, quirky person and not, in essence, the human blanket wrap that she appeared to be from where I sat listening to the headmaster.

His name was Charles Kellerman Johnson, and it was apparent that even after a few years of being head of the Woodstock School, he hadn't come to grips with the place. He had been associate head, or something like that, at Phillips Exeter Academy, the high-toned prep school in New Hampshire, and somehow the gods had transferred him here, to one of the dozen or two still metabolizing, still breathing institutional hippie holdouts in America. There was the University of California at Santa Cruz, Bennington (maybe), Hampshire, Stowe, and Putney; and there was the Woodstock Country School. Charles Johnson, clearly, had been many times wounded by the place. He was too straight, too posh, too prep, and the kids, and probably the faculty, too, had gone after him. You could almost see the long darts wagging gently from his hide, the way they do on the bulls in the ring, before the matador steps in and begins his part of the festivities.

Charles did all the talking. He spoke of the history of the school; he spoke particularly of a time ten years in the past when the place was thriving; it was well before he'd come and before his sufferings began. I knew that if I could simply be quiet and nod sympathetically from time to time, the job would be mine. I sat still and stared at the young woman who had survived the Cherokee massacre at Bloody Creek; I nodded with sympathy and understanding at Charles Johnson. But why did I? As far as I knew, I didn't want the job.

Phase II had closed because of mismanagement, a horrible location, and the general indifference of western Massachusetts hippie-holdout culture to the sound of the disco beat. So I had acquired a new job, working as the assistant manager of a movie house. Management had informed me and the rest of the staff that the theater, which was located, like the Phase, in a shopping mall, was soon going to be transformed into an "art house." So I spent my library time boning up on Truffaut and Buñuel and Kurosawa, getting ready for my big new leap into film. That is, I was looking forward to sitting in the dark and watching movies. I had signed on to be an usher, and this, from what I could observe, was what ushers did when the supervisors weren't looking. But there was a problem: the bosses at Dahl Enterprises, the owners of the soon-to-be art house and about fifty other screens (as we in the biz put it) around Boston, had identified me as management material. Over the past month or so, I had been learning exactly what being management material entailed; it was not a pleasant thing, particularly at this corporation.

One afternoon, a few weeks before my big interview at Woodstock, my boss, Dillie, an enormous swag-bellied guy engraved all over with thug tattoos, including one that celebrated the nuclear demolition of Hiroshima, sent me off on an errand. The errand seemed simple. I was supposed to drive a van from Northampton to Boston. In the van were two heavy metal canisters, containing, in total, one movie. As I hopped into the van for what appeared to be an easy day of work, my boss gave me some final instructions. "If anybody, like, wants to stop you or something," he said, "like some car starts gesturing you to pull over? What you got to do is, you got to ignore them. You know how fast the van is." It was fast: they'd juiced it up for speed. "You just gun it, OK?"

Dillie was always gassing on about various inane matters—in two months working with him, I'd gotten his philosophy of life: "Get laid as much as possible"; "Make all the money you can"; "Don't take any shit." I had by and large stopped paying attention to him. Dillie was the muscle for the enterprise: after

I left, I heard that when one of the theater managers had absconded with a Saturday night's proceeds, Dillie had scoured Boston for him and finally located him in a hospital. Apparently he had owed money to some members of the Winter Hill Gang, and what he'd taken from the house in Roxbury that he managed—where *Shaft* seemed to be playing all the time—was not enough. Undaunted, Dillie supposedly visited his wrath on the guy's car.

Dillie did show me one resplendent move, though. It happened when I was assistant-managing the art house in Amherst, not far from Northampton: Bergman, Fellini, Bergman, Bergman. Mostly the job involved sitting in the tiny office and reading a book; someone else worked the ticket booth. For four days running, a new ticket taker, whose name was Elaine and who looked like the prettiest girl at the Mennonite prom, blond and straight-backed and serious, did perfect work. Each night, she came to my office with exactly the amount of money her ticket sales indicated she should have. This was surprisingly rare: I'd worked the ticket booth a few times, and though I was always in the ballpark, I only rarely hit it on the head. When I called Dillie on the fifth night to let him know that Elaine had gotten it precisely right five times in a row, he said simply, "Go out there now and fire her ass."

"What?"

"You heard me. Go out into the lobby, find her, and fire her."

"Are you crazy?"

"You know the answer to that question," he said. (This was a warning.)

But I persisted. I needed to know why. "Because she's stealing from us, that's why. Anybody who comes in perfect night after night is stealing. Now, don't make me come down there and fire her for you." This would not be in Elaine's interest or my own. So, in company with the manager, a preternaturally articulate guy who really did know something about film, I did as I was instructed. Elaine hit the roof like a rocket. She cried and screamed and begged. She declared her innocence to the moon and the stars. She demanded a polygraph. Finally, after an hour or so of soap opera, she went her way, leaving me feeling like a brute. But a few weeks later, her boyfriend confessed to me that Elaine had indeed been skimming at a steady but sure rate from the cash box. In fact, Elaine had been stealing things from about the day she entered the world. Dillie, who'd never met her, had called that one right from afar.

My trip to Boston was uneventful. Nobody pressured me to pull over, though a state trooper did gesture at me to slow down—I was a little spooked and going too fast. I got to the North End, the Italian section of the city close by the Boston Garden, and finally located the address, a hole-in-the-wall men's social club. I brought the film in and began yakking with a couple of the old guys hanging around the entryway. They were dressed, it seemed, for Sunday bocce with small snazzy hats, white shirts, and elastic bands around their biceps. They thought it was a riot that I didn't know what it was that I was bringing them. It turned out that the movie was nothing other than one of the sex scandals of the decade, *Behind the Green Door*, and they were set for an afternoon not of bocce but of porn-viewing pleasure. Was I aware, they wanted to know, that the Mob controlled the distribution of the film and that they were ill disposed to anyone else having or showing the movie? The old guys thought this whole thing very amusing. I told them about Dillie's takeoff instructions to me, and they asserted that in my place, they'd drive pretty fast back to Northampton as well.

A few weeks after the North End run, a letter came to my door from something called the School Service Bureau. The bureau was an outfit that located teachers and connected them with private schools: they specialized, it seemed, in servicing offbeat schools at unpropitious times of the year. I had registered with the agency at graduation, in part to persuade my parents that I did have a career and a future in mind. My kindhearted mother kept up my correspondence with the SSB long after I'd forgotten about the place. When the letter came, telling me about the job at Woodstock, I had about as much interest in a career teaching as in one as a professional yodeler. (I had been a "teaching intern" at a prep school when I was in college, and overall it was not a success.) But I had to extract myself from Dahl Enterprises, and it seemed a good idea to find a place more than an hour away from Dillie, who might take my leaving personally. Also, Woodstock was in Vermont, one of the last peace-and-love holdout states in the union. Vermont was like Xanadu to us in Northampton, a mythical nation-state where you could do pretty much what you pleased, though frequently in temperatures less than ideal. I decided to make my way north for the interview.

I heard Charles Kellerman Johnson's weak monologue— his voice had the sound of water trickling across granite— though I took in virtually none of it. I got the job. I took it. I wrote Dillie a long letter telling him about my lifelong hopes to teach, about all I had learned from him, and about my new job in California. I left Northampton with all my possessions in my still aerialless Ford and reached Woodstock at the beginning of June. Soon my troubles began again.

But the Woodstock Country School was something to see, and my first day on the job I greeted it with high expectations. It had once been a gracious Vermont horse farm, and it still had a subdued aristocratic quality. From Upwey, the classroom building, the land rose higher and higher into the woods, a many-voiced chorale of green. The land seemed to hold the classroom building and the library in the palm of its hand, proffering kind protection against the elements. The girls' dorm was a lush old farmhouse with a spooky name, Owen Moon House, which sounded like the place to hold séances, though rumor had it that Owen Moon was a missionary and surely would not have held with such behavior. The dorm where I was to be installed was snug, a bit dark, and had a firm, fortresslike feeling to it, a Dungeons and Dragons feel. I was elated that I was going to get out of the mongrel three-decker in Northampton and particularly that I was going to get away from one of my roommates, who was a charming enough person, but who expressed her pleasures at operatic decibels when she entertained gentlemen callers in her room.

I was told that Woodstock had something of a distinguished history. It had been around for about thirty years and had always gone its own way. It had been coed when few other boarding schools were. It had sustained a working farm where the students had labored, milking cows and baling hay and growing vegetables. There had been fewer social restrictions than at other places—the boys and girls could actually enter each other's dorms without calling down a half-dozen sanctions. Woodstock all along had had something of a bohemian air:

a lot of the teachers were hipsters—poets, painters, dancers, musicians, and wayward math whizzes—who were still together enough to teach very good, if offbeat, classes and to drive the kids to the dentist and doctor when need be.

The place had cruised for years as a happy and prospering enclave, but then around 1967, the world began to agree with the Woodstock Country School. All the strange things that the school valued—independence and the outdoors and the arts—were proclaimed to be supreme. For the Woodstock Country School, this was a disaster. Applicants came at the place in human waves. The school had to beef up its admissions office; the faculty grew. So many kids wanted to come to the school that its trustees, believing as those creatures in the Keats poem do that the "warm days will never cease" and that peace and love would be the way of the world for eons to come, did something tragic. They built a dormitory. The dorm—which was called simply New Dorm, in hopes that a donor would come along, plunk down a sack of gold to pay off its mortgage, and slap his name on the place—was a behemoth by school standards. It housed about seventy or eighty kids at full occupancy and had three faculty apartments. It cost a lot to heat, even when it was first built. After the oil embargo and the rise in fuel costs, it required a small fortune annually to keep the pipes from freezing.

That was actually all that was required during the time just before I arrived—keeping the pipes from freezing—because there were now not enough students to make use of the place, and it was empty. What had been the ultimate alluring boarding-school experience in 1969, seven years later was no longer. When I got there, the school was overstaffed, overbuilt, and way underattended.

Summer session was about to start, and there looked to be no more than 35 students around. (At its height, I was told, the school had held about 160.) Kids had left or were leaving; teachers were sending out their résumés, and the headmaster, as I clearly saw, was deeply unhappy. Why they were hiring someone fresh was a complete mystery to all concerned—my new colleagues looked at me as though I was some kind of gift box delivered to a building that happened to be on fire. I asked the man in charge day-to-day—the dean of students— what it was I should teach. He gave me to know that neither he nor anyone else really cared. He told me that I could simply hang around for the summer and get used to the place. I could draw a salary; I could have room and board. This seemed too good to be true, or at least too good for me. I decided to deliver a seminar on the works of Karl Marx, early and late.

The five students who sat around me at the seminar table had no interest whatever in Karl Marx, early, late, or middle. Their chief interest seemed to be sustaining a version of the four-day Woodstock Music and Art Festival, which had been held not in Woodstock, Vermont, but 150 miles away in Woodstock, New York, and had taken place a decade ago. They wished to sustain this festival, or an illusion of the festival, for as long as possible. Woodstock students sat in circles strumming guitars and improvising Native American chants. They smoked weed through most all of their waking hours. They lived in tepees or in structures called acorns, tiny modules so flimsy that the Big Bad Wolf could have sent them to splinters with a breath, or in rooms as cluttered, dank, and bad smelling as anything to be found in Weimar Germany. They swam naked in Buffy's Pond, ignoring the designated family hour, from two to three in the afternoon, when bathing suits were supposedly required.

(In doing so, they were brutally snubbing one of my new colleagues, a history teacher, a man of tympanilike girth, a true scholar who orated at length about family hour to the community, who read fat books and somehow got some of the kids to do so as well. He strolled around in a brown caftan; his wife and son, also amply proportioned, had identical brown caftans, and the family sometimes appeared in them simultaneously, creating a three-bears effect. He lumped his plate with the starchy German-style food that came from the kitchen—"It's like living near a restaurant, a free restaurant," he told me.) The Woodstock kids were an Aquarian trip. They thought my fixation on Marx and the 1844 economic and philosophic manuscripts was insane, even when I took to wearing sunglasses to class.

With one of these students, I made the mistake of falling in . . . the single word to cover this feeling does not exist in the dictionary. Let's say, for now, falling into "erotic fascination." But to see Lilly Jenkins drop her clothes into a tie-dye puddle on the sand in preparation for a wood-nymph slide into Buffy's Pond was to be taken captive completely, at least if you were me. That Lilly was glowingly tanned, with red hair so luxurious that one could almost get away with speaking of tresses, that she was voluptuous and walked in a manner that made you think of Eve making her way through the garden—this was only part of the story, though not a minor part. Lilly was what you might call a natural.

At Woodstock, I was the priest at the party. I was all of twenty-four years old, but I was a figure of authority. I had nothing to do there but teach my class and enforce the rules, such as they were. Underage drinking was against the rules, nominally; faculty fornicating with students was against the rules, more than nominally. It had happened in the past, and there had been scandals. Hanging around with students, intoning ersatz Sioux warrior chants, taking the occasional bong hit, and passing remarks about the only book everyone on hand seemed to have read, *The Hobbit*, was also not allowable: faculty-student dope smoking was verboten.

As to other diversions, I had to be in the dorm every night at ten to do dorm check. Sometimes there were some students around to check, sometimes not. Then, I was in the middle of Nowhere, Vermont, without many places to stray. I checked my dorm; I listened to Miles Davis's *Fillmore West* about a thousand times; I reread the classics of Marxist theory, dearly wishing that Pelops was on hand to hold forth on them, teach me new revolutionary chants, and prepare me for an egalitarian future that would also be the world's greatest rock-and-roll extravaganza.

The kids I taught seemed to range from monumentally to mildly stoned. One of them, called by all his pals Auto-Motto, had long hair and hipster glasses but moved—and more disconcertingly, spoke—like a machine. Auto-Motto was the brightest and most engaged kid in my class. Occasionally, when directly asked a question, he would respond, though what he said did not always touch on the question posed. Before class some days, I played a game with myself called Dentist or School. Would I rather be strolling to an hour appointment with the dentist or heading off to my seminar on Marx? Sometimes I'd have to stop and consider. Were we talking about a full root canal or only a filling, because if it was the filling . . . On top of having to put up with daily classroom doldrums, I was radically lonely: none of the other teachers were crazy about making friends; they were all looking for a life raft out. The thought of a new colleague on hand confused and mildly annoyed them. There was only one sinuous, glowing spot in this dank world, and it was Lilly.

I'm sure that when Lilly was a little girl, she was forbidden this and that. No more cookies, Lilly. Lilly, you've got to stay inside. Lilly, lock the gate and don't leave the yard. Such sentences must have been spoken. But still, in her eighteenth year, Lilly, with her tousled red hair and unfailing smile, had the presence of someone who had never been told no. She'd never been put upon by civilization, never curbed, never limited. She'd always simply been herself, and from the day of Lilly's birth, the world had looked upon that self and found it good—splendid, in fact. You felt that food tasted better to her than it did to other people; the sweet air was sweeter. The water that closed over her when she dived like a seal below the surface of Buffy's Pond was cooler, crisper. Part of the reason she was so alluring when she was naked was that she felt better naked than clothed, more herself. Nakedness was her natural state, so she preferred it. In conversation, she talked of herself. But she did so in such an innocent, unapologetic way, describing her affection, say, for the soaps or shampoos she favored or the kind of cotton sheets that felt most agreeable next to her body or the fine grain of sand she most liked to sunbathe on, that she was anything but boring. She could evoke pleasure in her listener simply by describing her own. As she spoke, I could imagine—no, I could feel—the overtaking joys of those cotton sheets and that luxurious shampoo. Lilly loved her body, not only because she thought it beautiful, but also because it gave her such pure pleasure. She talked about the joys of this or that encounter she'd had in the same tones she used for the sand and the shampoo and the sheets. She did not criticize things: she took pleasure in what she could and tried to keep her distance from the rest. She could write reasonably well, engagingly even, when the subject was herself. On other matters, such as the distinctions between Hegel's dialectic and Karl Marx's, she had less to offer.

Lilly could have been half as beautiful as she was and still have mesmerized me. I had come into the world, or at least I had come out of puberty, full of strong desires. My will—the word Lord Schopenhauer uses to describe our inborn charge of desire, our hunger for sex, power, prestige, and all the rest—was potent enough. I wanted and wanted: though what precisely I wanted was not always easy for me to figure out. What counts as desirable to a twenty-four-year-old who mistrusts all institutions and all figures of authority? By the time I got to Woodstock, I had already spent a decade, at least, figuring out ways to rechannel my raw energies so as to get what I hoped for, insofar as I could discern those things. I'd read a pyramid's worth of books so as maybe to make my way among the writers and high-thinkers. I'd pumped all that iron—time in hell before you're actually sentenced—to become something like an athlete. Though I'd come into the world not entirely lacking natural endowments, I'd still had to strain. I was always looking at myself not as a being, a completed thing, but as a work in progress. I was a slab of mud or, more charitably, a block of marble that needed a hell of a lot of sculpting. The sculpting was ongoing—how many other bouncers stand at the door of the discotheque and memorize Browning poems?—and I was always pushing forward. That process, as you might expect, created endless amounts of inner tension, tension chiefly between what was and what would be, or what I hoped would be. I was forever in a state of becoming, or if I wasn't, I was punishing myself for it. Then I would collapse in a state of indolence or protracted boredom. There were so many things I might want to be (writer, athlete, scholar). The gap between these things and what I actually could claim to be was a source of ongoing pain.

Lilly seemed to suffer no comparable pain. There was no being that she wanted to possess except the one that she had now. She wasn't dedicated to "writing a more authentic self into existence" in the mode of Jean-Paul Sartre and Simone de Beauvoir, two of my heroes at the time. But Sartre and de Beauvoir were—why mince words?—outrageously ugly. He called her the Beaver in honor of her capacity for work and also for her buckteeth; she might as well have called him the Toad, for he looked to be a crouching, wart-creating thing. It is, perhaps, the ugly (physically, morally, emotionally, what have you) who are the prime existentialists: appalled by their own being, they throw their lot in with becoming. They go all out for the *pour soi*, the "for itself," and denigrate the *en soi*, the "in itself." From the time Lilly was born, all those around her had gazed their fill and proclaimed that she was marvelous as she was, the perfection of *en soi*. Soon she joined them in their belief.

Is it hard to see what an allure Lilly had for me, even beyond her red-haired, blue-eyed beauty? She could never understand, much less adopt, the collection of pressures and counterpressures that I often was. And why should she? Granted, I sometimes quelled all the warring parts, through drugs or sports or good luck or the perfect job as a disco doorman, and then became tranquil, taking on the elegant indolence that I felt was my Oscar Wildean birthright. But it did not happen nearly often enough. When I was with Lilly, her naturalness rubbed off a little. Once upon a time, I had been His Majesty the Baby, too, and I must have recalled it, however dimly. (My mother used to rhapsodize on how stunningly beautiful a baby I had been, stopping strangers on the street, but in these paeans there was always an implied comparison to a current, less luminous self.)

At puberty, all of us get hit with a charge of zoombah—libido, will, juice—and it is great or it is small. Then we have to set about figuring out how to handle the quotient that we've been dealt. In women the hit of hormones can come with a flowering into beauty and with that beauty, a remarkable poise —a self-sufficiency that is a marvel to behold. Freud reflects, perhaps a bit cruelly, on the narcissistic woman (as though no narcissistic men ever have existed). "Strictly speaking," says the professor, "it is only themselves that such women love with an intensity comparable to the man's love for them. Nor does their need lie in the direction of loving, but of being loved; and the man who fulfils this condition is the one who finds favor with them." The importance of such women for the erotic life of mankind is very great, he says. For men will do anything—create empires, write epics, journey to the moon—so as to acquire their favors. Freud compares such women to cats, large beasts of prey, and even criminals and splendid humorists—creatures who do not really give a damn what we self-divided, care-ridden creatures think about them at all.

Lilly's presence was an inebriant. She got me mildly high. When I was alone, I could tell myself that she was prone to be lazy and self-absorbed. But in person, she was perfection, and without even being terribly flirtatious (flirtation is artifice;

179 •

CHAPTER 7 : SCHOOL DAYS (DEPRESSION)

Lilly was a natural), she fascinated me completely. I'm persuaded that she wasn't trying to bedevil me when she gracefully dropped her clothes into a colorful pool and lay herself down naked by the pond. She was being herself. She was doing what she, at that particular moment in time, wanted to do.

I thought of the poet Ezra Pound, a very distant relative of mine, I've since been told. When young, the great modernist lost his teaching job for consorting with a young woman at a boarding school. Marry her or go, they told Ez. He went. I would have been quite willing to lose my job at Woodstock for consorting with Lilly. But it was clear to me that Lilly wanted nothing of the kind. If she had, I would have known it. What Lilly wanted, she was immediately and guilelessly forthcoming about. I was not on the menu. She liked me, but she also tended to like anyone who liked her. Such people were manifestly right, joining as they did in the general assent of the universe.

Lilly was just about my only source of pleasure during that time, if you could call the feeling that she provoked pleasure. But as the days passed, our interest in each other waned. She grew tired of my incessant analyzing and criticizing. I didn't grow tired of her natural ease, but I did figure out that however much time I spent with her, nothing would change for me. I would always be an anxious, unfinished project, looking forward with a mix of hope and dread—looking for the ever-elusive *it*. She would always have no real interest in the future, for there was nothing for Lilly except extended Now.

I did not like being a failure, but a failure was what I—along with the Woodstock Country School—was fast becoming. I couldn't get anywhere with Lilly. My class, with Auto-Motto as head boy, was a flop. Every day I offered unedited, unedifying monologues followed by questions that hung in the air like clouds of skunk perfume, slowly dissipating, never addressed. I was teaching only one course, a chaired university professor's load, yet I could not do any writing. I felt that I had nothing to write about, despite the fact that I was living at the heart of the empire in what they called the American Century. I was reading, but nothing of great import—I'd become an expert in the consumption of magazines. The library had all the back issues of *Esquire*, and I was making my way through them. In time, my teaching fodder, the classics of Marxist thought, barely got a glance; I skimmed them, hoping to rekindle old rants of Pelops's, which I usually could do.

I was ferociously lonely and tried on a few occasions to connect with Pelops on the phone. Dave's telephone on 187th was out of commission or simply went unanswered. I even tried catching the people's tribune downtown at his parents' house. In time, I found that I had to give it up.

But in my imagination, I told Pelops about my plight. I went on and on about the dismal life I'd acquired through no fault of my own. (I blamed it in part on *Behind the Green Door*.) But Pelops was hardly sympathetic. One did not go to Pelops Kazanjian for comfort: analysis was his game. When I told him how miserable I was at Woodstock, he went on for a while, quoting Marx about "the idiocy of rural life" and denouncing latifundia in general. He told me much the same thing as he had about Bennington a couple of years before. Then he issued his verdict. "You're not depressed," he told me, "you're alienated." I was a potential déclassé Marxist intellectual who had tried to relegate himself to lotus land. I was sojourning with the pleasure-seeking rabble. I was trying to dodge the dialectic, ducking the inevitability of historical struggle. No wonder I was feeling empty. I had great energies, and after my period of tutelage with him at the Uptown Center for People's Studies, I had some scientific knowledge to my credit. I should have been organizing workers and writing books celebrating Marx and Engels, not preaching the gospel to the sons and daughters of our class enemies. "Your students," Pelops, asquat on the judgment seat, decreed, "are too guilty about their families' ill-gotten wealth to go to a real prep school, and they're too lazy to get out and fight against hegemony. They are human phlegm. Abandon them. Return to New York. Create revolution." Then Pelops (my Pelops) added a final kick: "I'm sure there's a female involved in this: the bourgeoisie has no more effective trap than a babe. Beware, Homer! Beware!"

Alienation can be redeemed, or at least Marx and Engels think so. There's revolutionary action or (maybe) getting out ahead of the curve of history, philosophizing. Alienation is a sociopolitical condition. Depression is—well, what the hell *is* depression? No one quite knows. Suffice it to say, I felt it crawling up and over me like a shadow. I was someone who wanted to want things. But Lilly didn't want me at all; I couldn't write a word; and as to the larger question, the question of finding that elusive state where mind and body and spirit and imagination and all the rest got into play, I felt that I was a few thousand light-years from reaching anything like it. Maybe I was asking too much of the world. Maybe I should have cut back demands, the way workers do when a strike isn't going well. But I did not know how to do that. Young people like me want everything, yet they have no idea just what *everything* is or might be. Maybe depression sets in when the energies go stagnant. It rises up when you've despaired of getting what you want or, much worse, can't find anything worthwhile to desire. The response I imagined from Pelops was far from irrelevant, though it came down to me in my mind—as it would have in life—with the same measure of tact that Pelops employed when he marched down Park Avenue singing his songs about killing the rich. Stop desiring *as an individual*, was what Pelops had been trying to tell me all along. Begin to desire things from a new vantage, as a member of a group. Want something not for yourself, or not for yourself only. Want it for others. Want it, maybe, for humanity. Then go help get it. "You will learn, Homer," Pelops whispered in my inner ear. "Homer, you will learn."

Things got worse. It was unnaturally hot in Vermont that summer, and I felt like a corpse, out baking in the sun. I had trouble getting out of bed. I was beginning to approach the condition of Auto-Motto, who no doubt had his reasons. The school was collapsing and was taking down with it all the metaphors about peace and love and harmony and understanding. The kids never bathed. They did little schoolwork. They spent the day high as primates; at night they really trashed themselves and sometimes slept where they fell. Give them freedom, Burke and Johnson and a whole grand line of conservatives had said, and they will revert to the condition of beasts. They seemed to be reverting. The headmaster became ever harder to find. The teachers didn't spend an unrequired moment with the kids. The school buildings, which were supposed to be scoured by the students on Friday afternoon, during something called All School Clean Up, went foul and then beyond foul. My class became a charade.

One afternoon late in July, I casually remarked to the headmaster that it might be good for the kids to have something to do on Friday night other than get high, and higher, and pass out. What did I have in mind? I wasn't sure, maybe some live music. The headmaster, astonishingly, came to life. Did I know of a band? Could I bring one to the school? There was money—lots if it, it turned out—stashed in the student activity fund, and as such it had to be used for, well, student activities, and preferably for activities more edifying than buying acid, taking it, and stumbling around in the woods for three days, which is approximately what one of the kids, speaking at one of our interminable school meetings, suggested that we do.

It turned out that in summoning a band to play at the Woodstock School in that summer of 1976, I gave the entire student body a resupply of something that had gradually leaked out of it like air from a great tie-dyed balloon, something of which I was then bereft and that all human beings badly need. I gave them something to look forward to; I gave them hope. Word spread around the school about the coming of the band, and suddenly the students (even Auto-Motto, slightly) came to life. What was the band called? The truth is that they were called nothing at all. The band I had in mind was simply a group of guys, with a female singer, who'd gone to U Mass and who got together from time to time to jam.

Occasionally, almost by accident, they'd pick up a gig. In their most recent manifestation they'd played for a van owners' get-together in a great field somewhere in the wilds of western Massachusetts. Guys who'd spent what seemed a lifetime painting their vans and turning the insides into super-plush playpens apparently reveled in one another's company. Once a year, they assembled, got high, heard some music, and did whatever it is van owners do to achieve satori.

My pals did not get off to a good start with the vansters.

"What do you want to hear?" Jimmy bellowed to the assembly. "How about some Van Morrison? Could you dig some Van Halen? How 'bout a little Martin *Van* Buren?" It took them a while, apparently, but in time the vansters realized that they were being insulted. In not too long, they drove my pals off the stage—which was nothing but the roofs of three vans parked in kissing distance to each other—chanting, "Shit, goddamn, get off your ass and jam."

What's the band called? the Woodstock kids wanted to know. At first, based on the van-convention debacle, I called them the Pariah Dogs. Outcast dogs play a role in the novel I was trying to read at the time, Lowry's *Under the Volcano.* But then, on the off chance that someone might own a dictionary and the yet more obscure possibility that he might use it, I changed the name to the Bro-Dogs Band, with apologies to Robbie, the singer, whose voice actually held the music together.

Where had they played, the Bro-Dogs Band? I had heard they'd been at Watkins Glen. I knew for a fact that they'd been at the Seatrain show at the University of Massachusetts. (They'd been sitting beside me on blankets, gaining altitude all afternoon from a mess of modifiers and watching two young women in close proximity take off their plaid shirts, take off their skimpy undershirts, take off their bras, and move this way and that.) When the word began to spread at Woodstock that the Bro-Dogs had done a set with the Dead, I did nothing to set things straight. Rather I relayed to the kids for the thirtieth time one of the few raps of mine they actually seemed to listen to, about the time Jerry Garcia and I bumped into each other backstage at a show and took note of the fact that we were both wearing the same kind of sneakers, Adidas, white with green stripes.

What did the Bro-Dogs play? They played rock-blues-funk-pop-jazz, with an occasional side order of klezmer. (This was true. Jungle Jimmy, the band's musical all-star, was a flash on the clarinet and supported himself in part by showing up at the odd bar mitzvah and tooting away.) Fantastic!

How much would it cost? Not a nickel would come out of any student's pocket. Fantastic one more time: this was going to be a free concert, like Woodstock. You see, I allowed the kids to understand, inventing freely, this band's been broken up for a while—drug problems, rehab, creative conflicts—and they're looking for a small venue to try out some new stuff and see if they can recover their vibe. There had been dissension. This happened all the time in the music world. I mentioned Crosby, Stills, Nash, and the ever-temperamental Young. Heads nodded.

The reunification bit took over the kids' imaginations. The band is getting back together again! Some of the students actually made signs in celebration of the fact. (That summer the kids generally made nothing, unless you counted bongs.) They were developing an almost parental interest in the Bro-Dogs (Pariah) Band. They were going to help effect the reconciliation. They were going to be grade-A fans.

The band and its associates arrived on the day of the gig, a Friday, at about noon, seven guys and three women, and—*Fuck family hour!*—soon we hit the pond. We were bigger, hairier, louder, had more booze, had smoked more weed, splashed bigger waves, and were somehow more naked than the piddling kids, who were driven to the edge of the pond. It was Hippie Heroic Circus at Buffy's Pond, with naked horse fights and body tosses, and extended back-floating and sky-gazing with soft phallic flowers gently floating. The band and associates got toasted in the sun, then went off to get high, then got toasted again, then got a little higher. Iced-up beers appeared, and were dispatched. By eight o'clock, as the sun was kissing the tops of the Vermont greenery, we'd skipped dinner, drunk all there was, and were not at all collectively sure where we might be and what ought to come next. We were lying around on the floor of my dorm apartment. A few of the students moused their ways to the door. "Is there going to be a concert?" one squeaked.

"Got any acid?" one of the pariahs asked.

"He's kidding," I told them. "Big joker." The kids dispersed.

At around nine o'clock, we staggered into the Bro-Dogs' van—which, given the state of the inhabitants, should rightly have been called Rip Van Winkle—and rolled down the hill to where the entire school waited: the students and teachers and administrators, and the kitchen help and maintenance guys and even the sorely beset money man, who was going to have to lay on this crew what may have been the last liquid assets the school possessed. They had been there for well over an hour and a half, polite as nuns, waiting to see if the rock extravaganza was going to materialize.

Set up! I had set up equipment for the best of them and for the worst. I'd hoisted amps and strung power cords for Pink Floyd and Alice Cooper and the Dead and the Allman Brothers, and I slung the amps of the Bro-Dogs Band with authority. I gave orders. I pointed and humped. My part was soon discharged. But then came sound check and the checking of the sound check, and so on. It was ten-thirty before anything approaching an actual song could be heard upstairs in the classroom building of the Woodstock Country School. Song? Songs? The band actually did know a few. But they had planned to learn quite a few more, maybe a dozen, during the time that they'd lost bacchanalizing at the water hole and semirecovering on the floor of my apartment.

So mostly they jammed. They made it up as they went along. The Dogs were drunk and stoned and tired and though opulently talented, this night was not their night. They honked and groaned and sludged and stopped and started again. They sounded more like a traffic jam in Boston than a jam band in Vermont. Someone could have been blowing a policeman's whistle through the performance. It would have fit in fine. It would have neither added to the sound nor detracted from it. At around midnight, I did what I'd done at about twenty other rock shows, indoors and out, I balled up a T-shirt, pitched myself on the floor behind the biggest amp they had, pushed the shirt under my head, and tumbled into sweet sleep.

I awoke sober, which was a mistake. It was cold and dark, and the Bro-Dogs and their associates were breaking down the amps and the PA system. All the students were gone, and no one was talking.

The band came back to my apartment and crashed. Jungle Jimmy slept for ten hours on my floor and then awoke revived and rewired, like a freak infant Hercules. By early in the afternoon on Saturday, the acoustic guitars were out, and a low-key jam was starting. Our voices were whispery. No one had much to say about the night before. At around two o'clock, in mild, discreet defiance of family hour, a few of us strolled up to the pond and immersed ourselves, in search of self-cleansing. By about seven that night, the Bro-Dogs Band, holding a fat check that I'd found slid under my apartment door, was on its way back to western Massachusetts.

Monday morning, I trundled down to the classroom building to get my comeuppance. The first person I bumped into was the headmaster, who had been making himself astonishingly present lately. "Great work the other night," he said as we passed in the hall. But then what did he know? All rock no doubt sounded the same to him. It sounded bad.

"Incredible," said Scott Buller, a wiry guy with electrified red hair. Scott was the school's guitar maestro. "Blew my mind," he sighed.

"Are they coming back?" This was Auto-Motto talking, Auto-Motto who on principle almost never spoke. That day, in homage to the dude who had brought the spirit of Janis and Jimi and Jim to the Woodstock Country School, the kids in Marx: The Major Texts actually conducted something like a discussion. I was a hero, a Bill Graham, a rock impresario like none other around. Even Lilly took a passing, complimentary interest in the band.

What pleasure had I brought? Not the pleasure of music, or not much of it. I had brought the pleasure of myth. I'd brought a freaky underground band with counterculture credentials, a band that evoked the Dead and the Stones and Woodstock, the real Woodstock. The kids wanted the endless dream of a world that was creative and amazing and alive: they wanted it to go on and on. They wanted disco and Gerald Ford and stagflation and pricey oil to go the hell away and more freak music to get itself made and played. They wanted the sixties dream that they'd inherited from their older brothers and sisters to be alive everywhere in the world, not just in some precious little copycat tooled-sandalwood pot-storage box of a school. They wanted their tepees and their mescaline to connect with something bigger, no matter how bad that something might sound in its immediate manifestation. (Blow a whistle! Go ahead!)

They wanted what they recognized as wild and true life, and I had provided a little bit of it for them. In the vicinity of Woodstock, Vermont, for just a little while, I was a King of Rock and Roll.

8

WOODSTOCK II

(vocation)

"If nothing comes, then nothing comes, this isn't exactly the enchanted forest." The line from my college roommate's commonplace book came to mind as I looked over the situation at Woodstock. If Woodstock ever had been the enchanted forest—enchanted by the spirit of 1968 and all the rest—it surely didn't look to be so any longer. The dorms at the school were turning into slums; the kids were becoming obstreperous trolls; the faculty was disgusted. Things were so bad that at one point the remaining teachers met and sent a delegation to the bank to ask if we might borrow more against the school's foreclosure value. Much had already been borrowed. Things were at such a desperate pass that my colleagues fingered me to head the delegation. I was told to ask for more "front-end loading" until we got back up and running again. The banker had all he could do not to break out laughing. He could see that the place was heading down the tubes. A few big ski hills had opened near the school over the last decade, and visions of transforming the dorms into condominiums no doubt did the Hustle (or the Bus Stop) in his head. We came back and told the school all about it: some of the kids wept. They were already in dismal spirits. The night of the Bro-Dogs had been a brief spark, but nothing had caught fire from it. Well, if nothing comes, then nothing comes.

But this time, enchanted forest or not, something did come. Mickey came. "Cat named Mickey came from out of town / Been spreadin' a new dance all around." I loved that song the first time I heard it and—why lie?—I still do. Mickey, true to the spirit of pop-rock, brings something fresh to town, a new dance called (of all things) the hand jive. To me the lines evoke a brassy, road-tripping hustler-prophet. But sometimes Mickey's what you need; sometimes a little hand jive is what the witch doctor ordered.

The cat named Mickey who came to try to save the Wood-stock Country School—and my prospects for doing something more with life than floating naked at Buffy's, pining after Lilly, reading more magazines than books, and writing *nada*, *rien*, nil, and zip—was then traveling under the name of Peter Engle, and he came from way, way outta town. He came from Brown University and the Wharton School (a business school, a festering free-market swamp!), as well as too many commercial ventures to name. He drove a Mercedes, or soon would, and paced the earth in big strides, as though he owned the part of it he was traversing or was seriously contemplating a down payment. An Aborigine who'd never left the outback would have recognized him as an American immediately.

Engle suffered from a condition that makes people highly suspect in all academic establishments and sometimes excludes them outright: he was handsome. Unfairly, blondly, with shocking blue eyes and a made-for-the-movies voice, the guy was good-looking. He looked like the cowboy who owns the herd, like the forty-year-old test pilot whom the others gape at; on his worst day, he looked like the guy who plays the surgeon on one of the afternoon hospital soaps. He had, or seemed to have, insane confidence. When you were around him, you sometimes felt that you were in a movie: he made life feel bigger than life. (That sparkle and flash that the Bro-Dogs and I had momentarily struck was Engle's nearly constant element.) Where he went, fireworks popped and fizzed, and people said "awwwwwhhhhh." He was clearly a big deal and a hot shit, and I disliked him immediately.

How did this guy come to Woodstock? He was the chairman of the board at another school, Stowe, and Stowe was considering dumping their own physical plant and taking over our poor, depleted skeleton of a school. They were going to relocate to our site: a guy about my age, wearing hiking boots and a weathered look, came to look over my dorm apartment to see if it might suit him. Soon I'd be tossed out onto the dirt road. But at the last moment, Stowe balked, backed away, and said no. Engle leaped forward to say that he'd gladly take over at Woodstock, provided he could be both headmaster and chairman of the board of trustees. (I think he wanted to stay on as chair of the board at Stowe, too; he probably also wanted to be captain of their soccer team.) He said he'd jump-start our school. We needed money? He knew where money was. For his services, he'd require about forty thousand a year in remuneration—I was making about seven, with room and restaurant-style board thrown in. But he made promises, this Engle. Things were going to roll: he'd get it all humming.

This cat named Mickey would help us discover America one more time.

Mickey had a modus operandi, a way of going at the Woodstock situation. He possessed a philosophy of life, though I'm not sure he ever drew it from a book. To Engle, it seemed, a healthy human being was someone who wanted things— good things in the long run, OK. But sometimes just wanting *something* was the first step. He understood the attraction of not desiring anything, but also understood that it was usually a form of pathology. One of the Gallic shrink Jacques Lacan's most dire diagnoses was that "the patient desires to have no desires." This happens because having desires makes you vulnerable in a dozen different ways. You may get disillusioned, you may get stiffed, but maybe most disturbing of all, when you admit you have desires, you're admitting that you're not complete in yourself right now. There's something wrong. This question of wanting things had particular weight at Woodstock. A hippie, or a certain sort of hippie, was someone who lodged a protest against the Machine by claiming to want nothing, or to want very little. Gimme a patched tepee, an Indian name, and a few grains of rice. I'll get by. ("I *will* get by," the Dead would later chant.) But was this not-wanting a matter of coherent policy? Was it philosophic, or was it all based on timidity or maybe on the desire to seem in perfect control? Engle was interested in these matters. He wanted to know.

So he summoned me—he summoned all of us—to his office. It was a sunny fall morning when I walked into his sanctum. The place had changed from the day of my conversation with Charles Kellerman Johnson. The walls of the office were now heavily colonized—*decorated* might be the wrong word—by a variety of images. It seems that the new headmaster had let some of the kids loose with cans of paint, so on one wall there was a mural coming into being. On another wall, there were drawings by an artist I'd actually heard of, who, Peter mentioned, was something like a personal friend. The old desk was still there, but Engle seemed to have replaced the chair with an American grand-pasha executive throne. It was contoured precisely to his back—maybe it had been custom-designed—and looked like the exoskeleton of the king of the beetles. The woman whom I'd seen out the window the first day, the one who evoked the burnt-down campfire, was gone; the mush and semigarbage and green plastic coffee cups had been taken care of, and the autumn sun was up smiling in the sky.

Engle sat behind his desk with his royalist chair slung back and his feet up on the walnut surface. He was wearing boat shoes, insanely droopy socks, and an outdoorsman's shirt, anarchy red. He bade me sit down and then stared at me with the icy blue eyes, as though he were looking at a strange book; he didn't want to read the book so much as he wanted the book to pipe up and explain itself, the more succinctly the better. We exchanged no small talk. Engle had no small talk. To him it was like the small change that sometimes came drizzling out of his pocket when he was sitting down; he rarely noticed it departing, and he sometimes didn't bother to pick it up. He demanded to know what it was that I had in mind for the rest of my life. He demanded to know what I wanted.

"Why do you care?" I asked.

"Because whatever you want," he replied, entirely composed, "I'm here to help you get it."

Who did this guy think he was, Aladdin's genie? Had I

inadvertently rubbed a magic lamp and brought this top-gun glamour-puss to life?

Playing for time, I told him that I didn't altogether understand what it was he was talking about. I said I figured this was a school and we were here to teach something to the kids, however many of the thirty-five characters now in attendance cared to learn anything.

"Bullshit," he said. "Nonsense. That's a ridiculous theory of education. What are you, a social worker or something?"

I made a question mark with my face.

Engle then gave a brief speech. He informed me that a school worthy of the name was dedicated to the development of everyone who was part of it: students, sure, but also teachers, maintenance staff, kitchen people—the works. A school was all about everyone bettering himself, and by his own standards.

"So Edmundson," he asked me, "what do you want?" I ran a quick inner audit: I wanted Lilly; I wanted to be a famous writer (though without the trouble of writing); I wanted to know something (college, it seemed, despite its many charms, had actually taught me little). But instead of answering or just crouching low and hoping not to get hit, I swung my shield in his direction.

"What do *you* want?" I asked.

He was ready for this. He looked up at the sky, as if to make contact with the deities above—for perhaps he took himself to be one of them, though of a minor stature, to be sure.

"Jesus, what *don't* I want? I want to be a better father. I've got two sons. I'm divorced. I'd like to find a woman and fall in love and get into a half-decent relationship. I'd like to stop thinking so much about money; I've got more bills than you can believe. (I can't even tell you what my monthly nut is.) I'd like to be more comfortable in my skin. Shit, I'd also like to have some fun."

Was the boss supposed to talk this way? He was 40 years of age or so, which in my book was close to 111. Why wasn't he acting like a grown-up? Which is to say, why wasn't he pretending that he'd solved all his problems, that he'd punched the right selections into the jukebox, and that all the right tunes were coming out?

But there was more to come. He checked in again with the kindred sky powers. He became reflective. He said that he was maybe in the process of figuring out that he was a person who was in the world to help other people flourish— he used that word *flourish*. He figured if he could manage to do a little of this flourish-enabling here at Woodstock, then maybe some of the other things he hoped for might begin to take care of themselves. "Who knows," he said to the ceiling, "stranger things have happened.

"So Edmundson, now that I've bared my soul to you"—the soul would be bared often and bared to many in the months to come—"tell me one thing that you want."

I told him that I wanted to be a good teacher—shit, maybe I wanted to be better than that—maybe I wanted to be great at it. Where this came from, I can't tell you. I wasn't *aware* of feeling that way. But as I came to learn, Engle was often a sort of truth-creating machine. He concocted an atmosphere in which you said what you felt even though you never knew you felt it.

But there was a problem with this good-teacher, maybe-great-teacher business. The school had a history of spectacular, legend-producing teachers of English, and it was becoming pretty clear to all that despite my amazing coup with the Bro-Dogs Band, I was not to be one of them.

The guy I was replacing, the last in the line apparently, was named Andrews Fuller—Andy, a blond Californian who said he was forty-five, but appeared to be thirty, tops. He looked like a surfer (and was); he walked with an astronaut's bounce; he had a gentle-as-an-altar-boy voice. When he talked, he sounded like an adolescent in prayer. Andy had been brought to Woodstock by a former headmaster who firmly believed—and he was not alone in this—that Andy was the best high-school English teacher in America. He was paid about $15,000 a year, twice the salary of most of us, and was not required to live in the dorms. He had a place out in the Vermont hills, which he'd apparently built himself. You could see cougars from the back porch.

A few days before the fall term started, a week after Peter Engle arrived and took over, Andy invited me into his classroom and in his sweet voice told me that he had had it—though not so much with the kids or the school or even the administrators. He'd had it, apparently, with reading. He was unable to look at a page of print. When he opened a book and tried, he felt nauseous.

So he was going to quit—quit and become a full-time carpenter. He wanted me to know this before anyone else, because he was giving me his classroom, where he'd installed built-in bookcases and which had a view out onto the fields where, when Andy felt like it, he would go cross-country skiing between classes. He was also going to give me all of his books: he had a splendid library, which he'd begun during his undergraduate days at Princeton and built while he was in grad school at Brandeis, studying with Philip Rahv and Irving Howe. I was overjoyed about the books. It was like someone busting open a treasure chest and letting me have it all. But I was terrified, too. How was I going to live up to Andy's standard? I asked him as much. "Oh, you will," he said. "But try to do it in your own way. Don't try to be like me. *I'm* even tired of trying to be like me." And then he walked out the door of his sun-basted classroom. He stayed at the school a while longer, a few more months. But I knew his secret. Any day, he would be walking out, and I would be taking over as *the* Woodstock Country School English teacher.

I told Peter about my anxieties, though I kept Andy's secret out of the conversation. He looked down at his floppy socks. One iota of elastic less and they would have fallen off his feet. "So why do *you* want to be an English teacher anyhow?"

I had a dozen answers ricocheting in my head, but I understood that none of them was the true one. "I don't know," I said.

"You'll probably never be that great at it until you do know. But until then, I'll bet you get by."

I saw some truth in this and said as much. "Maybe you're a little like me," he added. "I've always wanted to be an artist of some kind. But you see, I'm not that crazy about making art. I just feel like being an artist. It comes with a lot of perks."

Then he asked me if I fantasized much about the girls at the school. I said nothing (and nothing and still more nothing). He drew in a deep breath, checked with the deities ceilingward, and I became sure that he was going to tell me about his own mental operations in this regard. I said no, sure, good-bye, good-bye, I have to go to class.

• •

My classes were not going well. I was not Andrews Fuller or Dave Hersey or Bill Balchman or any of the others in the line— -the students could recite their names the way kids at other schools (different kinds of schools) could recite the names of the kings of England—who strode up and down the halls of the classroom building dispensing light. The most gifted student in my senior English section, Leanne Darling, walked into class on the first day, cleared the books off a top sector of the bookcase, wedged herself up there, above my head, and went to work on a crossword-puzzle book. She did this from one end of the class to the other. When I asked her a question about Shakespeare—our focus for the term— she always knew the answer, though she spoke like someone dreaming a pleasant dream. Then sometimes she'd ask *me* a question: "Four across, one down. Bites like a dog." I never knew the answer. Leanne worked very rapidly and must have completed a dozen puzzles per class. She was what T. S. Eliot— Andrews had given me a book of his essays—might have called the class's "objective correlative": she summarized its concentrated essence of feeling in regard to me.

Meanwhile, Peter passed through the school like a sort of human torch: some things he lit up and illuminated; others he seemed simply to set on fire. For in those early days of the school's supposed rebirth, Peter loved doing two things. First of all, he loved getting people to tell him, and themselves, what they wanted in the world. In general, this made people happy. My closest friend-to-be there, Ron O'Mara, arrived at the school sometime after I did and told Peter that he wanted to be an artist of note; Peter promised to get him out of dorm duty, find him a studio, and find him time to paint—all of which he eventually did. When one teacher went to Peter and told him about her desire to grow herbs in a manner called "hydroponic"—whatever that was—Peter took an interest. When a maintenance guy let the new head-master know that what he most wanted was to get a trailer for himself and his wife, who had worked in the school kitchen for twenty years, then bum around the country doing odd jobs, Peter got on board and began drawing up plans. (The guy eventually did it, too.) When a kid wanted to build a guitar, Peter found him a guitar maker nearby to apprentice with. It turned out that the guy also built and raced bicycles and taught French; thereafter we had some French classes. So Peter brought fire, lots of illumination.

He was into being Zeus, but so far he was a pretty good Zeus, as long as you came up with the right tributes. The trib-utes didn't take the form of dull obedience or ass licking: Peter didn't like those things. You had to be spirited. You had to pipe up and say in clear terms what you wanted in life. When you did that, Peter could get on your side with a vengeance.

Peter strode around the school with his anarchy-red shirt and sky-blue eyes and then, in time, a neckerchief, either fastened around his neck or hanging a bit foppishly from his back pocket. Ron and I agreed that the hanky was a good index of Engle's mood. When he had the thing in his pocket, all might be reasonably serene. But when it appeared around his neck, it was cowboy time, and you got what you got. Then he hiked the halls, making declarations, midwifing dreams, and, as he never tired of saying, "giving people *juice*." Dispens-ing juice was part of Peter's answer to almost every human problem. Was a student failing math? "Give 'im some juice." Was he fighting with his parents? "Give 'im some juice." Was he mourning over a lost girlfriend? "Juice!" The recipe was juice, juice, and more juice. Was a kid smoking too much weed? (That really wasn't against the rules: the drinking age in Vermont then was eighteen; the pot-smoking age seemed to be about twelve.) If a kid was wandering around the school lonely and wispy as a cloud, clearly he was doing too much weed. Then: juice! Juice was energy, concern, interest, affection, libido, zoombah: juice was (dare one say it?) love.

We owed this juice to each other because, as Peter said a few quadrillion times, we were not just a hatching of individuals, running around randomly, everyone for himself. We were a community, too. We were a clan and we were a tribe. We were family. And a community was a place that thrived by taking care of its weakest members. We had some weak ones, too. Peter knew that we needed money to keep the school going, which meant getting more students, which meant, ultimately, not always being excruciatingly picky about who we took. If you had the money and wanted to come, you were likely to get in. But, truth be told, if you had no money and also really wanted to come, Peter would figure things out. He once took a girl's horse in lieu of tuition, then let her ride it every day when she came to school. When she graduated, as I recall, she took it home with her.

One kid Engle came up with was Paul Bradley. I first encountered Paul when he was standing in front of his dorm, trying to fly a balsa-wood airplane. To test the wind direction, he slid his thumb into his mouth to wet it (for an instant he looked like a contented infant); he withdrew the thumb, reluctantly, then stuck his forefinger up to feel the direction of the breeze.

His *parents* had said that he was hopeless, a loser. They didn't drop him off at Woodstock; they dumped him. He was the weakest of the tribe Peter called the Weaker Kids. On the subject of these kids, Peter was relentless. We gathered every week for a three-hour faculty meeting—three hours if you were lucky—and we discussed every student in detail. The Weaker Kids got the most time. (They needed the most juice.) Paul Bradley got more time in these meetings than anyone else. Peter kept asking questions about him. What subjects did he like? None. Was he passing anything? No. Had he made any real friends? Don't be ridiculous; he spends all his time smoking weed. To which Engle replied, "Of course he does. He's deprogramming himself from all the shit he's had to take. He has to clear some space. Stay with him." And then we all said in unison, with our varying degrees of weariness, mild derision, impatience (and hope, hope): "Give him some juice!"

At one community meeting, Peter let it be known that the growth and development of kids like Paul Bradley were not exclusively the business of the faculty and headmaster. The students had to pitch in. Why hadn't a kid stepped forward to tutor Paul in math?

The good students—there were some of those—were furious. "We paid to come here," they howled. They quoted the sum. It was high.

Peter was furious back. "Screw your money," he told them. "We're individuals, it's true. We've all got our dreams for ourselves. We're also a community. We're not leaving anybody behind. We're all responsible for Paul"—who was wrapped in a blanket, looking like the school icon, the extinguished campfire—"and we're responsible for Morning Thrush"—yep—"and Sarah and John"—all of whom were also sitting there in various stages of composition and decomposition.

"We *are*," Engle said, "one body, and anyone who can't buy that has probably got to get outta here." Hisses and catcalls came from the going-to-Oberlin, going-to-Berkeley crowd. That they had to *look* at Paul Bradley and his ilk was bad enough. Now they had to consort with him?

The faculty was placed on high alert: the Weaker Kids must not be abandoned. And the privileged few had to join up and help. No excuses tolerated. (We are one body.) About two months later at a faculty meeting, we came, for the umpteenth time, to the case of Paul Bradley. "How's he doing?" Engle asked. His intonation indicated that this was a question that was perpetually new, perpetually packed with the possibility of producing a surprising answer. We groaned collectively; or rather, all groaned except Dell Parini. Parini was the science man—he was a barrel-chested guy from Jersey with a beard down to his sternum. "We had a test in biology yesterday," he said. Parini's tests were known to be ferocious, and in grading them, he gave no quarter. "We had a test on all the material so far," he said softly. "And Paul didn't fail it." The place went shithouse. Then Dell added what was for him a major endorsement: "I think, just possibly, Paul's going to be alright.

"Oh, another good thing," Dell added. "Leanne Darling, right?" This was the girl who perched herself above my English class doing the crossword puzzles. "She just got into some school, Johns Hopkins I think, to study biology."

There was more applause, from everyone but me. "Hey, I'm college advisor," I hollered. "Why don't I know about this?"

Dell looked at me with great patience. "I think she arranged to send the forms in herself. She said something about you being new to the job and maybe not knowing how to do it."

• •

So Peter Engle, human torch, went around providing rare illumination—glowing light. But he could also enjoy igniting things. He seemed to like a good conflagration. He went around interpreting people. He'd get a line on this student or that, this faculty member or that, and then he'd let fly. "I think that something in you actually wants to be just like your dad—you know, you've got a leadership thing, a power thing." He said this—or something like it—to Raffish Wolf, the most prominent among the Woodstock Indians, the kids who had somehow gotten permission from Charles Johnson to build wigwams outside and to live there summer, winter, spring, and fall. They roamed the woods and bathed when the spirit took them. Raffish's father was a long-term employee of Dow Chemical, working out of Washington, dispatching representatives throughout the world to do who knew what, but surely to do things that did not accord well with living lightly on the land, conducting sweat lodges, and bellowing "Ho!" whenever someone said something vaguely Native American–sounding at community meeting. He was big on fathers, Engle was, and he would—no charge—readily offer you his gut feeling on the unresolved state of your paternal situation. (As to his own paternal complex, he had plenty to say—just ask.) On the subject of Wolf Junior and Senior, maybe Engle was on to something: Junior was a very self-serious young dude, as well as a smart and talented one—he played a mean guitar; he was boss of the Indians and seemed to lord it over whom and what he could. Still, wasn't Peter stepping over a boundary here?

"What if you drop an interpretation like that on a kid and you turn out to be wrong?" I asked him. "Can't that kind of thing be bad?"

I had to admit that Engle had an uncanny sense about how to do this interpretation/intervention thing. He'd tumble down into the dark room of your psyche, clumsy and disoriented enough. But often he'd find the right alley and send a sixteen-pound piece of business rumbling down it. *Whap* went the pins, spinning and tumbling in all directions. But what if he was wrong? On this matter, Engle nursed a strange belief. When he was wrong—and Engle admitted that this *could* happen—the unconscious of his beneficiary would simply reject the information, as though it were a letter sent to the wrong address. *Not for me! No one by that name living here!* But if the info stuck, if you remembered it, couldn't get it out of your head, and especially if it pinched, then there had to be something to it. When we held a reunion, twenty years down the line, there were more than a few kids—now no longer kids, but strangely adults, about my age—who had what they called "serious issues" to take up with the headmaster, who though into his sixties, looked most resplendent.

But usually when it came down to the confrontation thing, Peter had a simple mantra. "I'm just trying to unblock him," he would say. For Engle's money, virtually all human beings were blocked, with brutally (though archly) constructed dams upstream in their psyches, preventing their pure energy—their juice—from flowing free. If you'd walked a conservative sage, an Edmund Burke or a Samuel Johnson, through the halls of the Woodstock Country School, he would have suggested that a little more blockage might be a good idea. There was altogether too little dam construction going on. For one thing, the kids were disposed to cavort in the altogether, not only at Buffy's but wherever and whenever they liked. One day the new math teacher, a genial, soft-featured guy, assigned the kids a tough geometry problem and then stepped out for a drink of water. When he returned, the students were contemplating the intricacies of the side-angle-side theorem, yes. But they were completely unclothed, naked as a mess of trout in a pool. The new teacher pretended not to notice that anything was amiss and proceeded calmly through a forty-five-minute exposition of SAS. For doing so, he was shot into the Woodstock cool teachers' hall of fame.

Nudity was a major motif at Woodstock. There was Buffy's Pond; there was the math class; there were multiple random streakings by both boys and girls. There was also Engle's reaction to an idea, mine, about having a lecture series featuring eminent people with something to say about education. "Sure," he said. "But I won't pay them, because they'll learn more from us than we ever will from them. And also, we'll want them to stand up naked when they talk." Why? It would incline them more to honesty, Engle felt. "Will the school be naked, too?" Engle didn't know. He'd have to think about that.

Engle kept pressing me about the teaching business. I hadn't yet gotten down to basics on it—hadn't made myself naked. Why did I care so much about getting good at teaching? Why did I want to stand out?

I told him about the great teacher I'd had in high school— Franklin Lears. Lears came to our prole high school in the fall of 1969, and he opened us up. He showed us new ways to see the world, new ways to see ourselves, and not all of them were pretty. He gave us the plans and the hacksaw to get out of Plato's cave, the hall of illusions, pieties, and prejudices most of us inhabited.

"Why did he do that?" Engle wanted to know.

I told him what I then believed to be true. Because Lears was a good man, because he was generous, because he wanted to make a contribution. He was a liberator. As Emerson said of the true poet—but I held it true of the genuine teacher as well—he was free in himself and he wanted to make other people free, too. To which Engle said, rather peremptorily, "Bullshit."

What? A shrine of mine had just been desecrated. Someone had pissed in the sacred chalice. What was I supposed to say?

"The reason," Engle said, "that you may never amount to much as a teacher is that you have a dumb view of what makes a teacher good, or anybody good at anything."

"Well, Socrates," I began. I was about to start in about the sage's dedication to pure knowledge. I was about to start in, period.

Engle looked at the ceiling, no doubt petitioning the fellow deities for some patience.

"How do you know?" I asked him. "How do you know who I am? What do you know about me?"

"Hey," the maestro said. "It's fairly obvious, isn't it? I mean you're not exactly a saint. You're a hustling intellectual. Yeah, that's what I'd call you. You're a hustling intellectual. You want to help people. OK, fine. I think you really do love your students. If you didn't, I'd try to get rid of you. But you've got some ambitions, too. You want to get on in the world. You may even want to be a big deal of some kind."

"Fuck you," I said.

Engle laughed. He was the only boss I ever had that you could insult without infuriating, which made me unfit ever to have a real boss again.

"Why don't you go think about it," he told me. "Maybe that's what you're about, the hustling intellectual thing. Why don't you go give it some thought?"

I made a *hummphhh*ing sound far too venerable for my twenty-four years and stormed from the office. Engle's was probably the most stormed-from office in America at the time.

"I'll tell you this." His voice followed me out the door. Like Hamlet, Engle always liked to have the last word. "You're not one of those pure good types, assuming there might be one or two in the universe. I mean the way you look at Lilly. Lucky you can't eat her in a gulp. Maybe you . . ." But I didn't stay around for the rest. I had to go to class and teach Shakespeare and watch Leanne, Ms. Johns Hopkins, on her perch, and try to help her figure out seven across, and steam some more about the "hustling intellectual" business.

"Cat named Mickey came from out of town": what such cats often do is make trouble for you. But he had nailed me, or at least part of me. He'd knocked down quite a few of my pins. On some level, I believed that growing up meant becoming someone who was *good*. This state was something that I both resisted and yearned for. *Good:* I wanted a place, a groove, some respect. *Good:* but Jesus, how boring, how small, how wearisome—how antithetical to the teeming One Life within us and abroad, the best spirit of drugs and rock and the movies and even of Pelops Kazanjian. So all of this I had to mull over.

It was hard, as the days passed and the world outside the school changed, not to see Peter Engle in contrast to America's supposed primary boss, recently inaugurated Jimmy Carter. After the departure of Nixon and his shadow, Ford, America seemed to have wanted slippered tranquillity. The nation voted for bland and got it. Carter aspired to placate all, ask nothing of any, and inhabit both sides of every divide. He was a president for dull times, but unfortunately the time of his administration was anything but dull, as crisis followed crisis, until things peaked with the taking of American hostages at the embassy in Iran. Carter seemed tired; he assumed that after Vietnam, Watergate, and Nixon, America was tired, too, and he hoped never to have to wake anyone up and ask for anything. Engle understood that what makes a consequential leader is the ability to ask things from people that they think are above their heads, to give them some spirit (juice) and help them pull through. In his small kingdom, Peter Engle understood that leaders lead people to new places, at least if they're going to be worthy of the name.

Engle went on developing his school, which he now sometimes took to be without parallel in the world. (One of the trustees, a friend of Peter's, told me that he liked to give Peter support, but not too much. Why? "If he gets too much support, I'm afraid he'll wake up some morning and decide to annex Austria." But in fact, Engle kept his imperial aspirations pretty well in check.) Peter concentrated his ideas; he concocted principles. There was juice. There was unblocking, community, flourishing; there was nakedness. Each of these would strut a few weeks on the school stage, and then, though it would not be retired exactly, it would recede a little toward the wings to be replaced by another protagonist. But the concept that maybe best epitomized the school, at least to Engle, and the one that I in many ways was most moved by, was a simple one. It took the form of just a few words. "We deal openly here." That meant no posturing, no bullshit. It meant that though you gave the kids what guidance you could, you showed yourself to them as a flawed individual, in the process of development, too. You didn't pretend you had it all right and understood all things. You represented yourself to them as you took yourself to be: you dealt openly. Surely this open dealing had its merits. But maybe it also had something to do with the demise of the school.

While I was teaching English, fuming at Leanne and working out on Engle's remark about my being a *hustling* intellectual, Peter was spending a large amount of his time doing what a headmaster of such a teetering, tottering place had to do: he was raising money. One of Peter's coups, scored during his first months at the school, was to maneuver himself into the presence of Laurance Rockefeller—not Larry, Laurance. Rockefeller had an estate in Woodstock. He was said to own the Woodstock Inn. He was said to have made sure that all the power lines in town were buried underground—he paid for it—because surface lines would have chafed his sensibility as he drove through his domain. He was, it seems, a bit like a landowner out of Tolstoy: Woodstock was the estate; its residents were functionaries and serfs. Or at least that's how local gossip had it. Peter had charmed his way through a secretary, a manager, and a few factotums and gotten a meeting with the magnate himself. And then—maybe he'd given Laurance a much-needed jolt of Woodstock juice—he'd emerged with a commitment of $50,000 to pay the school's outstanding debts for the year. Peter also left with an understanding that the fifty would appear annually in the Country School bank account for the next two years, maybe more. Fifty grand in 1977 would have paid almost all the faculty salaries: it was a major hit.

But then came the day that Laurance and his wife, Mary, visited the school. I wasn't there for the actual encounter, but the story was told time after time, perhaps most memorably by Peter himself.

Peter had set the stage adroitly. It was summer, a Saturday afternoon, and not many students or faculty were around. He'd handpicked a few teachers and friendly trustees and maybe some students of the more or less presentable sort and decided that because the Rockefellers had some aesthetic interests (those hidden power lines), he'd treat them to an exhibition of paintings done by students and alumni. The show was set for three o'clock in the amphitheater, a moss-grown enclave by the girls' dorm. But the sky was cloudy all morning, and then, early in the afternoon, the rain came. It rained wildly, a temper tantrum of a storm, as though some god had a grudge against the school—and no doubt a few did, the pure, abstemi-ous gods, Apollo and Artemis to start. (Dionysus, on the other hand, probably loved us dearly.) No outdoor art show today: so the group went off to Peter's house on the edge of campus.

By about four, the Rockefellers still hadn't materialized. No doubt they weren't coming. The Woodstock gang exhaled collective relief: they weren't going to have to face the pluto-crats after all. They could go back to their favorite diversion, being themselves. Shoes and socks got taken off—but nothing more than that. Somebody popped open a flagon of fourth-tier wine, and the paper cups came out. They were filled. They were emptied. They were filled again. Peter and com-pany admired the paintings, quaffed the fourth-tier, and made remarks on the unreliability of the rich.

Over the crest of the hill on the road that led to Peter's house rose the great black jaws of a Cadillac. It hove softly, like a yacht, into Peter's front yard, doing what no automobile heretofore had done on the premises of Woodstock: making his pale green Mercedes look shabby. Soon the doors were opening and the lord and the lady were stepping out onto the gravel. Apologies were made, explanations proffered, shoes surreptitiously slid back onto feet of dubious cleanliness, and soon Laurance, turned out in a charcoal suit, and his wife, in a mutedly elegant summer dress, had taken their seats and begun to get to know the tribe. Would the visitors care for a cup of tea? We'll have what you're having, Mrs. Rockefeller said, as she had no doubt said about thirty thousand times before, for not to have what the hosts are having is the height of bad manners. So they got the paper cups and a few splashes of fourth-tier from a jug so large that the pouring could have been a two-man operation. Loaded up, the Rockefellers commenced sipping, with what grief inflicted on their usually much-flattered taste buds can only be imagined.

Mrs. R. began to take in the scene. From her straight-backed chair, she stared down at the crush of hippies on the floor and on what Peter called his bordello couch, a crimson velvet number, more at home in New Orleans than in Vermont. She saw piles of books. She saw papers. She saw genial, hippie-school headmaster mess. But then—what have we here?—her eyes landed on the stack of paintings. This, after all, was what they had come to see. She and her husband had something of a collection. She talked about this, with an assist from Peter. She spoke of her interest in, no, maybe even her passion for art. Let's have a look. Peter, always obliging, stood up and began to show the visitors the paintings, one after the other. Some of them were abstract; some, a tad gamy. But basically things were going well: this Woodstock School, despite what the locals may have said about it, was apparently a womb of creativity, an offbeat Athens teeming with Krazy Kat invention. Lady and Lord R. seemed not unimpressed.

One particular piece of work caught Mrs. Rockefeller's

eye. "And who is it that painted this?" she asked. Peter gave the name of the artist, who had graduated from the school not long before. But at this point, Peter, who was not generally a religious man, surely began to pray. He hoped, hoped, hoped. Mrs. Rockefeller asked the question that was not to be asked. "And what is this interesting painting called?" Peter knew that the title was written on the back. But he knew very well what the artist had named the work. He did not need to be reminded. He did not have to look.

Surely he wanted to plead ignorance, to throw himself on his knees and ask that before he answered this question, the $50,000 would be assured for one year more, or two or three; or perhaps he simply wanted to jump into a hole and begin shoveling loam on top. But there was the business about dealing openly, about nakedness, about confrontation, and about standing up for yourself. There was the business about telling the truth. And there was also the fact that Peter seemed to like to throw dust in the air sometimes to see if it might be magic dust, or merely sand, as everyone else thought.

"The painting," Peter said, "is called *Asshole Sphinx*." It became spectacularly quiet. No one had much to say. Mrs. Rockefeller worked the pleats of her skirt for a while, paid the whole collection a surpassingly mild compliment, but expressed no willingness to see more. She was suddenly uninterested in encountering the work from this new provocative salon, Woodstock. After the silence, there arose highly amiable, then ridiculously spirited conversation. Then came the moment of parting, and Mr. and Mrs. disappeared into the great black galleon, its trunk no doubt loaded with sacks of gold, doubloons, and pieces of eight. The sacks were untouched and now, for us at Woodstock, untouchable. Later, when Peter stood on the welcome mat, the great man was not available to receive him. Peter trudged away, the disappointed suitor—but alight with principle: We deal openly. We tell the truth and go naked, too. What we had there on display that summer day was an Asshole Sphinx—elastic, fantastic, orgiastic, and ours—and we'd proclaimed as much to the world. Now we were broke.

It was probably a little after I heard about the Rockefeller business that I began coming to terms with Peter's bit about my being a hustling intellectual. Maybe Peter's display of whatever the hell it was that day with the noble Rockefellers helped me out a little. Maybe it was dealing openly, maybe simply telling the truth, the way my mother had been instructing me to do since I had ears to hear. But I started looking at myself in a new light; maybe I started figuring some things out. I'd been hoarding some high-toned ideas, it seemed. When no one—my conscious self included—was looking, I probably took them out and polished them and marveled at their sheen, then hid them away again in a strongbox far back in my psyche. I was going to be pure, unselfish, and true, the way I imagined Frank Lears to have been. I was going to be some kind of pedagogic saint. I was going to be humble and self-effacing, putting the students first and always shoving myself to the back of the line.

But that wasn't working. I did have some hustle in me. I did have some ambition, and maybe more than some. I saw now that I was always going to be a half-assed teacher unless I was getting something out of the deal myself. I mean more than the paycheck and more than the gratitude of students to whom I'd done my duty. So to begin with, I began teaching what I wanted most to learn. I was going to be a writer?

Good. Eliot, in one of the books that Andrews had left in the hand-tooled bookcase, had informed me that the only way to amount to anything in this regard was to get the whole of the Western tradition into my bones as quickly as I could. So I began teaching to educate myself. I taught Shakespeare, sure. But I also got to Milton and Chaucer in Middle English, and even to Spenser, a poet who may not have been taught at such length in any high school before or since. If we didn't dispatch all of the *Faerie Queene*, we came close. When the students said they hated it, I told them what Northrop Frye had told me in an essay on the poem: "I never met anyone who *used to like* the *Faerie Queene*." Once you're in, you're in, and a few of them actually made it there. And as to those who didn't, well, eventually we'd be on to something else. I wasn't going to let the students get in the way of my education.

My humane side, such as it was, didn't disappear. I still wanted to do for those kids something like what Frank Lears had done for me. I wanted to give them a chance to grow up again, guided by books this time, rather than just by Mom and Dad. I wanted them to be made free, as I felt books had made me free, and as I believed they continued to do. (Though to be sure, such freedom has its costs.) Emerson said that if he understood that a man was coming to his house with the express intention of doing him good, well then, to update the idiom, he, the Sage of Concord, would run like hell. But, I thought, if someone were coming up the road to profit himself and me, too, and if without me, he could do nothing, then I'd await him gladly. I became to my students a bit like that man rising over the crest, a self-interested idealist peddler with his bag of goods. For without them, I could not do much. I said things in class, thought things in class, which

I never could have on my own. They were my muses, those unwashed, weed-sucking, often golden-hearted sixties left-overs, and I needed them to inspire me as much as they ever needed me, though I made it a point not to let on.

One day in my novel class, I was giving Faulkner a hard time for making Benjy, the idiot boy in *The Sound and the Fury*, into a Christ figure. He's innocent, he's holy, he's thirty-three years old; there's more along these lines. Then what I'd believed to be one of the more thought-free stoners in the class raised his hand. He told us that maybe Faulkner knew what he was up to. You see, Benjy was absolutely harmless, much like Jesus. He had no aggression in him. When other characters encountered his uncanny innocence, they became intensely and illuminatingly *themselves*. The violent became more so: that was how it went with Benjy's brother Jason. The compassionate—like his sister Caddie—showed their natural love. Benjy was a touchstone in that with no particular effort, he distinguished base metals from gold. He gave people the chance to know who they were, which is in a way what Jesus tried to do. I hope that Kerry never forgot his interjection—I haven't. I loved it because it marked real growth for him—I'd never actually known him to *think* before; but also I loved it because it served my purposes. It taught me something I didn't know.

Some time later, rummaging around in Freud, I read a remark that underscored what I discovered there at Woodstock. What makes a great surgeon? the master asked himself. Well, there were some predictable factors. To be a good surgeon, you had to be smart and to know a lot. You had to be disciplined and energetic; you had to be an ace at getting out of bed at three-thirty in the morning and showing up at the operating theater with your mind as clean and sharp as your tools. You had to be humane, too. You had to want to do something for your patients, and you had to be able to talk with them before the operation, so that they knew that you cared about them and that you desperately wanted things to go well. All of this went without saying.

But to be a good surgeon, you have to have something else, too. On some level, you have to enjoy the hell out of cutting people up. There's a sadist in the best of them, Freud bet. They like power, and they like making incisions: it all gives them a rush. Everyone who achieves much of anything has probably got a nasty enough side. But the trick is that rather than burying the worst, the way that most people do, with the effect that it's always popping out sideways, those who truly flourish manage to integrate their nastiness with their other more benevolent parts. You've got to give the devil his due.

Later I came upon a line in Emerson that compressed the wisdom of the surgeon story in a savory nut: "Your goodness must have some edge to it,—else it is none." A real surgeon's goodness would have an edge to it, no doubt about that.

So what was the teacher's edge? My plan was simple: I was going to give the kids all I could, but I was going to exploit every chance the place gave me to develop as I wanted to. I was going to get myself an education—a real one this time— and get paid for it. I was going to draw more from the Woodstock School than any full-tuition paying customer. I'd work for the kids, but they were also going to be working for me.

"We are one body here," Peter said. He said it with the implication that anybody who didn't really want to take that seriously, who didn't like it, could scram. Though we were also, he gave us to know, individuals: we had our hopes and ambitions, our powers and promise, and in those things, we were each distinct from the other. The genius of Woodstock, when it was working, was that it functioned like a great jazz band. Everyone got to take his solo. We all got to run up and down and through the notes with the support and often the admiration of the others. But everybody also played a lot of backup. You had to know how to help construct a runway that the person next to you could use for takeoff. Your solo was better because of the reinforcement other people gave you; your spirit felt calm because you weren't a loner, but one of a group. And (odd paradox here) being part of a bunch, subsuming the self, made you more an individual. I can't say for sure how that worked—the business about being *both* part of a collective, tucked in sometimes like a koala in its mama's pouch, *and* being a striding individual, one of a kind—but it did work. For a while, we had a real school there. We had quite a run.

And I? I guess I can say that I had my *it*. Is it possible that human beings, once they're sheltered, clothed, and have gotten something passable for lunch, chiefly want two things? One of those things is the sense of community. We yearn for belonging. We want to be part of a group that's bigger than our mere selves and that cares for us. We want to help others and to be helped by them in turn. We seek a world infused with what Saint Paul calls agape; Lord Buddha, compassion; and Confucius, benevolence.

But here's the trick: we want something else, too. We want to be number one; we want to be first in power or in strength. We want everyone to look up at us with awe. From Homer on, the lure of the heroic individual has been unrelenting. In my few years knocking around in the world, I'd tasted a little of both of these things. I got a hit of the regal, striding feeling back there in school, listening to the Rolling Stones. I'd felt it when Duggan Senior riffed on about the glories of the free man in the free market and exemplified those glories after his own fashion. I'd taken a snort when I was the doorman at the disco and those ladies loved me (a little). I'd felt it when the piece Duggan and I wrote—about bathrooms, no less— caused its little stir and our names were on the lips of the coolest writers at the coolest of publications, the *Village Voice*.

But I'd experienced the other thing, too. I'd been taken over by the feeling for the One Life within us and abroad, in all its tenderness and ferocity, sitting on my hillock whacked on LSD. And I'd felt it when the crowd opened like a rogue blossom under Grace Slick's spell: we can be together. I'd even felt the sense of wholeness—of one body—when Pelops, my rogue Socrates, went on about the workers and the peasants and the fact that fucking people over so you could have a third vacation house wasn't fair, damn it, and it was gonna end.

When you push one of these drives—the heroic or the compassionate—to the complete exclusion of the other, trouble usually spills over the brim. Without a reserve of compassion, the hero becomes a brutal killing machine, like Achilles in his wrath. But without a jolt of *thymos*—the *desire* for distinction— people can go slack. After a while, uncompromising hippies sometimes acquired the consistency and appeal of moldering white bread. That was the story for half the Woodstock Country School denizens before Engle walked onto the scene.

What I learned at Woodstock was that most of the time in individuals, these feelings, the compassionate and the glory-seeking, go around colliding with each other. Socrates said man is the rational animal; Aristotle, that he's *zoon politikon*, the political animal. But I'd dare to say that we're the animals in whom the drive for glory and the urge toward compassion are always alive and most of the time in conflict. Most of the time, but not always. Sometimes you make some luck for yourself, and at Woodstock that's what I did. I got to strive for my own aims, and I got to play a part in making a bunch of people into a unified whole where love wasn't absent. I struggled to develop as a writer and thinker, *and* I got to pass along the gifts that I'd received from people like my marvelous teacher Frank Lears.

At the tiny, inconsequential Woodstock School, bright, bright kids ended up on the way to med school, and poor straggling creatures, forked things that everyone had given up on, pulled themselves together and got some friends, stopped toasting themselves charcoal with drugs, passed their courses, and got the high-school degrees their parents had given up on ever seeing. These were sometimes parents who for all purposes drove by and slid their kids out of the front seat like bound bodies in a gangster flick, hollering out the window, "Good luck with her. She's a loser." We didn't buy their shit about losers. We stuck with everybody to the end. And we had some fun, too. In a small space, we created a revolution you could boogie away to if you wanted. Pelops, if he ever could have figured out how to leave New York, might actually have liked it there.

But the end did come. Oil costs got higher, and Vermont winters are cold. The culture turned more and more against the idea that education was about what Nietzsche enigmatically but accurately suggested it was: teaching someone how to become himself. And the legacy of *Asshole Sphinx*, which in its way had to be one of the more expensive paintings in

America in the 1970s, costing as it did as much as a quarter-million dollars, stayed with us. Laurance never came through with another dime. When the school began to crumble, we all bowed, spoke a few lines, and made the best exit we could. I went off to graduate school at Yale, which had its blessings—it was an intellectual feast like no other I've experienced. But compared to Woodstock, on those days when we really had it going—well, Yale was a little short on soul. (*Lux et Veritas*, Light and Truth, is a beautiful motto, and Yale often lived up to it, but can *Lux et Veritas* really compete with Nakedness and Juice?)

After the school closed, Peter went on to lead a calm, reasonably quiet life, especially considering his capacity for striding around, making pronouncements, and looking at things as though he owned them or was contemplating a down payment. I still hold it against the world that Peter doesn't have a big desk at the Harvard Graduate School of Education, where he holds forth in his way, grandly hitting and trivially missing as he was wont to do. He should be there now talking about juice and nakedness and creating one body and dealing openly: there should be a line outside his door. And I suppose I hold it against the world, too, that Pelops Kazanjian isn't the boss of some grand collectivist-minded think tank, singing a gentler but firmer version of the song about the bourgeoisie, who truly can be blind mice in their way, and concocting, along with the ghost of Emma Goldman, a revolution that you can dance to. (I've run with some clever company in academe, but never with anyone I thought had much more intellectual zoombah than Pelops Kazanjian.) It all came out differently.

But maybe I've done a little to spread their word. Maybe

what Pelops and Peter Engle and also Duggan and Duggan Senior and Grace Slick and the rest, my Kings (and Queens) of Rock and Roll, taught me will have some use to others. And maybe they'll spread it around a little themselves: for in the making and telling of stories there can be a kind of virtue.

Maybe compassion and glory are the potent twin aspirations of the soul. But perhaps there's another strong spiritual hunger that besets human beings, not as potent as the first two, but not weak, either. And that's the hunger to think about things. I'm talking about the need to look at life and ponder and try to make some sense where none is apparent. I mean doing one's best to figure our experience out in a clear-minded, detached way. (Plato says that thinking—not courage, not compassion—is the preeminent thing in life. I'm not sure he's right, but maybe, maybe.) In any event, the chance to reflect on the best moments in my young life (and a few of the worst) has been a stroke of great good fortune. I'm glad to have had the shot. And for now, that's *it*

acknowledgments

Gratitude abounding to Jennifer Barth, Gillian Blake, Chris Calhoun, Elizabeth Denton, Michael Pollan, Jason Sack, and Alex Star.